Young Bucks

HOW TO RAISE A FUTURE MILLIONAIRE

by Troy Dunn

THOMAS NELSON
Since 1798

NASHVILLE DALLAS MEXICO CITY RIO DE JANEIRO BEIJING

Published in Nashville, Tennessee, by Thomas Nelson. Thomas Nelson is a registered trademark of Thomas Nelson, Inc.

Thomas Nelson, Inc., titles may be purchased in bulk for educational, business, fund-raising, or sales promotional use. For information, please e-mail SpecialMarkets@ThomasNelson.com.

Library of Congress Cataloging-in-Publication Data

Dunn, Troy.
    Young bucks : how to raise a future millionaire / by Troy Dunn.
      p. cm.
    ISBN 978-0-7852-2185-2
    1. Parents—Finance, Personal. 2. Parenting. 3. Responsibility in children. 4. Entrepreneurship. I. Title. II. Title: How to raise a future millionaire.
    HG179.D859 2007
    649'.6—dc22   2007020629

Printed in the United States of America
08 09 10 11 12 QW 10 9 8 7 6 5

Every page of this book is a tribute to my father, Roy, who taught me that it's OK to dream big. His entire life has been a steady pursuit of dreams, ideas, and ambitions. The "little boy" that still dwells within him is a continual source of inspiration and drive in my daily life.

I also want to embrace my mother, Arliene, as she is the one who showed me how to laugh and skip right through adversity. No matter how dark the hour or how hopeless a situation may appear, Mom always demonstrates that humor takes the sting out of almost anything.

Mom and Dad,

I.L.Y.F.E.I.L.Y.F.A.

Contents

Acknowledgments   vii

Introduction   ix

One—Millionaire Mentality   1
Think Like a Future Millionaire's Parent

Two—Mentor Magic   15
Set the Stage for Change

Three—The Millionaire March   27
Identify Your Child's Business Talents

Four—Business Building Blocks   39
Pave the Path for Success

Five—The First Meeting   49
Light the Learn-to-Earn Fire

Six—Business Begins   59
Start the Start-up

Seven—Big-Buck Businesses   71
Great Enterprises: Basket Case to Game Guru

Eight—More Big-Buck Businesses   85
Great Enterprises: Gopher Girl to Rent-a-Scrap

Nine—Even More Big-Buck Businesses   99
Great Enterprises: Shoot-for-Loot to Wonder Windows

Ten—Business Pitfalls   113
Sucker-proof Your Future Millionaire

Eleven—Sweet Returns on Passive Revenue   125
Make Money Do the Work

Twelve—YoungBucks.biz   135
Continue the Journey with Me

About the Author   145

Acknowledgments

THREE PEOPLE ARE DIRECTLY RESPONSIBLE FOR BRINGING this book to reality. First, Jane Dystel, my literary agent, has expressed more belief in me than almost anyone else on earth who isn't a family member. Janice Billingsley, my extraordinarily gifted writing partner, invested almost two years and hundreds of hours into the birthing of this written work. And Victor Oliver, my editor, saw my desire to bless the lives of families and children worldwide and honored me by making me a part of the rich tradition of Thomas Nelson.

I also want to recognize the immense contribution that my seven beautiful children have made to this book by their own examples. Between them, they have started more than two dozen businesses and sold thousands of dollars' worth of goods and services—and they are all still under eighteen years old! (Another generation of little people blessed by what my father taught my siblings and me so many years ago.)

But most important, I want to point the spotlight directly at my eternal companion, high school sweetheart, and wife of nearly twenty years, Jennifer. As the mother of this incredible family we are raising, in addition to the full-time duties of managing such a large household, she has often been the one to run kids to town for "business supplies." She has stood in front of the grocery store as they sold their wares, helped them understand the importance of saving their money, and quietly urged strangers to "buy something" so our children would experience some level of success in their ventures. Along the way, she has continued to be supportive of me as I have been out in the world, launching my own companies—some succeeding, some not. Jennifer is truly the center of our family teeter-totter—the source of our balance. I have often told her how brilliant and beautiful she is, what an amazing mother she is, and how grateful I am to have her as my beloved bride. But being able to tell her that here, and to tell everyone who ever reads this book, is exhilarating and hopefully additional proof to her of my deep gratitude for the beautiful life she has given to the children and me.

Introduction

EVERYONE DREAMS THAT HIS CHILDREN WILL GROW UP TO be independent, successful adults, able to support themselves, their children, and maybe, if times are tough, even their parents!

Along with that dream is the deep and fervent wish that the children be happy.

Happy and rich—what's not to like?

These are loving and honorable goals, the same ones that I have for my own children and for the many young entrepreneurs I teach throughout the country as a successful businessman, public speaker, radio host, and writer of financial success and personal happiness resources.

Getting across to kids the message about thinking like millionaires is an uphill battle, however, and not for the reasons you might think (the difficulty of finding a good idea, the complexity of financing a business, ignorance of accounting, poor planning, etc.).

Instead, the toughest sell is persuading parents to believe in their children! I've found that while most kids are innately confident, their parents discourage them, beginning at an early age, from acting on their natural optimism and believing in their abilities, especially when it comes to money.

In my work, I meet many well-meaning parents who obviously yearn for the best for their children but whose outdated and ambivalent attitudes about money keep them from helping their sons and daughters prosper. Parents do wonderful jobs nurturing their children's academic, athletic, personal, and spiritual development, but when it comes to teaching their sons and daughters about financial success, these same parents are victims of out-of-date and even bogus myths about the financial world, which blind them to the skills their children really need in order to become wealthy and successful adults.

The good news, however, is that when parents realize that the key to their children's financial success is to reject these established norms and instead embrace their sons' and daughters' unique talents and teach them practical business skills, they become the best teachers possible. Further, their commitment to their children's futures brings father and daughter, mother and son together in surprising new ways.

How do I know this? First, because I'm a successful entrepreneur myself, thanks in large part to my own dad. I would not be where I am today without my father, a schoolteacher, whose lessons I drank in along with my hot chocolate at the Saturday morning "business meetings" we had at our local Denny's. And second, because of the times I've spent with my own children as we've worked closely together to help them create a business that would bring them both financial and personal satisfaction. The time spent with my dad and with my children on these projects has brought emotional rewards that can't be measured in dollars and cents.

Third, working for many years with children and their parents, I have witnessed the tremendous success achieved by young people whose parents have encouraged their abilities and given them practical business guidance.

For the past fourteen years, I have spent much of every summer speaking to youth groups throughout the country at conferences that draw over a thousand teenagers each, and I teach them all about business—ethics, marketing plans, brainstorming, fundraising, goal setting, and so on.

Twice in the last five years, I've been the keynote speaker at the annual meeting of the Young Entrepreneurs Organization (YEO), a worldwide, nonprofit group of nearly five thousand entrepreneurs under the age of forty, whose businesses have sales of at least $1 million. There I've shared my experiences of encouraging young entrepreneurs as well as motivating my fellow members.

More than four million people tuned in to my nationally syndicated business talk-radio show, *The DunnDeal Show*, which ran weekly from 1999 to 2003 on eighty-one stations throughout the country. Through call-ins and follow-up off the air, I helped thousands of entrepreneurs, young and not-so-young, create new businesses and improve those they had started.

My CD *Young Achievers*, which outlines how young people can realize their financial dreams, is a bestseller in the "Talks on CD" youth market.

As a result of my experiences, I've developed a simple and effective program to help parents change their attitudes about money so that they can become successful business mentors to their sons and daughters.

Now I want to reach out to a larger audience, parents who haven't been introduced to entrepreneurial thinking, or those who feel that their own lack of business experience or success renders them unable to help their children learn to think like a future millionaire. This is nonsense. All parents who love their children can teach them to become future millionaires.

Young Bucks: How to Raise a Future Millionaire will give you the information and confidence to help your children succeed in business. If you have picked up this book, you are already open to what I have taught many children and their parents—to reject the misguided information about financial success and to instead concentrate on channeling their natural talents into businesses that will earn them money and give them the confidence they will need to succeed. This is the best ticket to financial independence!

You will find here a straightforward, practical, and entertaining manual that first debunks a number of parenting myths that work against financial independence (such as giving your children allowances and thinking that children shouldn't have to "worry" about money when they're young—money shouldn't be a source of worry but of pleasure to kids!).

Second, I will help you identify your own children's talents and guide you in steering them to businesses suitable for their skills. This is a most rewarding process, one that will not only set your sons and daughters on the path to being future millionaires but also dramatically enrich your relationship with them.

Third, *Young Bucks: How to Raise a Future Millionaire* provides a number of very practical templates for easy, kid-friendly businesses that parents can introduce to their children so that they can start earning their own money quickly. These are proven enterprises with track records, undertaken by the many successful kids I have worked with across the country, and even by my own children!

Finally, information about my YoungBucks.biz Web site is coordinated with the book so that your children can join the

YoungBucks Club, learn about business opportunities, share ideas, and further promote entrepreneurship among children and young adults.

So please join me in teaching your sons and daughters to become future millionaires. You will be very glad you did.

ONE

Millionaire Mentality

THINK LIKE A FUTURE MILLIONAIRE'S PARENT

You and I are about to embark on a wonderful journey together—teaching your kids to think, talk, and act like future millionaires. You will find the experience surprisingly easy, as most kids are born with the ability to dream big dreams and are eager to succeed—the first two ingredients for great achievement. It will be extremely gratifying to watch your son discover that his own interests and talents, combined with practical business skills, can be the source of his success, earning him enough money to buy a new bike right now as well as preparing him to be a future millionaire. This is what I do for a living, and I can assure you that the rewards and satisfaction of helping children become independent achievers are never-ending.

But before we focus on your kids and their many gifts, we will begin with you, exploring your own attitudes about money and success so that you will be able to teach your son or daughter to think like a future millionaire.

The Parent Trap

Over and over again in my work with young people, I see the same tragedy unfolding—kids who are eager to become successful entrepreneurs and who have no doubts about their abilities to succeed, but whose parents, good people like you, unknowingly discourage them, beginning at an early age, from acting on their natural optimism and from believing in their abilities when it comes to money, the two leading characteristics of successful businesspeople.

While insisting that their kids work hard in school, supporting their athletic achievements, and generally loving their children, most parents, without knowing it, actively work *against* their children's future financial independence. By buying into some very pervasive, wrongheaded business myths in our country about work and careers and, further, by visiting their own ambivalence about money onto their children, they miss the opportunity to groom their children for financial success.

A tragedy? You bet, because what most parents are doing is the complete opposite of what they *want* to do for their children. No one in his right mind wants to deny his children the opportunity to succeed, both financially and emotionally. Yet I see this happening all the time in the seminars I conduct throughout this country and abroad.

No one has explained to parents that the most common path to great success is not what most people think—getting into the right college or landing a job at a big corporation—but is instead developing one's unique talents to create thriving businesses. Entrepreneurs learn this important skill early in their lives, usually from an adult who is close to them, and go on to build fulfilling and prosperous lives for themselves by creating their own businesses.

So before we begin to talk about your child and his or her talents, let's discuss the three harmful myths that block parents from helping their children become future millionaires.

Myth Number One:

A college education is the key to business success.

I'm the last person to disparage a college education. A good education teaches you to think critically, exposes you to knowledge, and trains you to be inquisitive and open to new ideas throughout your life. It can also prepare you for certain careers, such as engineering or accounting or medicine. But it is far from an automatic guarantee of business success or even a requirement for success. In some cases, it can actually put you four years behind the other runners in the race to achieve.

Many of the newer, most successful businesses in our country were founded by people who learned on the job rather than in college, including Los Angeles restaurant owner Wolfgang Puck, Microsoft founder Bill Gates, Miramax movie-studio head Harvey Weinstein, Apple Computers founder Steve Jobs, and *Vogue* magazine editor Anna Wintour.

In my own case, I won a football scholarship to college but left after one semester, because I just wasn't learning anything that seemed relevant to my life and my goals for success. Instead, I went to work, and by the age of twenty-four, armed with the confidence and experience I'd gained from my own childhood businesses, I was the CEO of my own corporation. On one occasion, I placed a help-wanted ad in the paper and got forty-eight responses within two hours, forty-three of them from people with college degrees. Here I was, a college dropout, in the position of deciding whether or not to hire a college graduate.

Please don't assume that teaching your son about business at an early age isn't important because he's headed for Princeton. Instead, encourage his business skills—he will be able to pay his own college tuition if he wants to go!

Myth Number Two:

A job with a good corporation will secure your child's financial future.

This was once true. Many of today's grandparents grew up with secure, long-term jobs at American corporations and factories and retired with gold watches and nice pensions. But as many people are finally beginning to realize, this is no longer the case.

Big corporate America is now a world of mergers, acquisitions, downsizing, and outsourcing. And for those who survive these upheavals and remain employed, the corporate workplace itself is often unfriendly and difficult, as employees struggle to do more with fewer resources, deal with cutthroat office politics, and work longer hours to produce a product of which they may or may not be proud. Further, all the while they are filling someone else's bank account.

Is this what you want for your child? Not likely. But while many parents now acknowledge that corporate America might not be the place for their sons and daughters, they don't know any alternatives. As a result, they stand silently by while their children march toward eventual financial disappointment.

One alternative is small businesses, often service oriented, which are the driving force of our economy. The approximately 23.7 million small businesses in the United States have generated 60 to 80 percent of the new jobs in this country over the last decade and employ half the country's private (nongovernment) workforce, according to the U.S. Small Business Administration.

And who's starting these businesses? They are entrepreneurs who have the skills, confidence, and determination to create something new and make it pay. Contrary to what many people think, these entrepreneurs did not spring fully formed into their success. Most often they were children, just like yours, who were taught by their parents, early in their lives, to identify their talents, trust their instincts, and use both to create unique, profitable businesses.

Your child will be no different, and maybe will be even more successful than other entrepreneurs, if you start now to teach him how to learn to earn. Give him the option to be his own boss when he grows up! He will thank you forever.

Myth Number Three:

Children should not have to "worry" about money when they're young. There's plenty of time to focus on finances when they're adults.

This line of thinking drives me crazy because, first, it assumes that money is scary, which is exactly what too many adults think and why they're so uncomfortable with their finances. On the contrary, I can assure you that teaching your child that she is capable of earning her own money is one of the most positive and empowering gifts you can give her. By helping her earn and handle money now, she won't ever have to "worry" about making money when she's an adult.

Second, this hands-off approach to money flies in the face of what parents do for their children in all other areas of their kids' lives. You encourage your children to take piano or dance lessons and play soccer or baseball when they are young to gain skills that they will enjoy and carry into adulthood. Why not give them the same opportunity to acquire financial skills that will pave the way to an affluent and secure future?

Mythmaking Mischief

To show you how damaging these myths can be to a talented young person, I'd like to tell you a story about a young boy I know, whose father, with the best intentions, is frustrating his son's natural inclination to success.

A few years ago, my sons decided they wanted to have a mural painted on their bedroom wall. They had a vision of a cool biker flying through the air on his amazing motorcycle, while an awe-struck crowd watched from below.

When I found out that paying an artist to paint a mural would cost about the same as wallpapering the room, which needed a new paint job anyway, my wife and I said, "Why not?" and I began looking around for an artist who could paint both lifelike people and shiny, impressive motorcycles, a combination requiring skills that seemed beyond most artists I asked.

Then one evening my son Trey appeared in the kitchen with a drawing of just what he and I had been looking for, a truly realistic, macho biker, whose fierce expression conveyed his determination to take his bike on a glorious sky ride. The bike itself was everything a boy would want—big and streamlined with every bell and whistle known to man.

"Where did you get this?" I asked.

"Paul drew it," he said.

I was astounded. Paul was his friend, a quiet thirteen-year-old boy with big brown eyes and an easy sense of humor. He was at our house all the time, and this evening he was spending the night when Trey and his brothers told him of their planned motorcycle painting.

He was obviously a terrific artist, and I thought we'd found the person for the job. But when I went upstairs to congratulate him and offer him the job of painting the mural for about $250, he said, "I'm sorry, sir. I can't. My dad would be really upset. He doesn't like it when I draw."

I couldn't believe what I was hearing. How could his father *not* like Paul's drawings?

When I took this news to my wife, she explained that Paul's father was frustrated because all Paul wanted to do was draw, to the exclusion of schoolwork, athletics, even dinner conversation. His teachers complained, his grades were poor, and his father blamed it all on the drawing.

In my optimism, I thought, *Well, maybe so, but surely I can talk to him and explain that Paul has a tremendous gift that should be encouraged.* Further, he'd understand that if he did support his son's talents, Paul would likely meet with great success. His self-confidence would grow, and most likely, when he was allowed to draw all he wanted, his schoolwork would improve as well. I just knew he'd be delighted to let him paint the mural. So with Paul's permission I brought the subject up when I drove him home the next day.

"Absolutely not," he told me firmly when I asked if I could hire Paul. "Giving him so much money to draw is exactly what we *can't* do. He has to learn to pay attention in school and improve his grades first—the last thing he should be doing is distracting himself by drawing. It's too impractical."

Paul's face dropped a mile at his father's words, but nothing I could say would convince his dad that discouraging his talent was just the opposite of what he should be doing.

Mr. Mercado, backed by our whole society's attitude toward raising children, is firmly convinced that the best thing he can do for his son is to steer him away from his "impractical" interest in art so that he will study harder in school. His dream for Paul is that he get good grades, go to college, and land a well-paying job. Then he will be successful, and his father will think he has done his job.

But he's dead wrong. It's clear that his son's passion and talents lie in his artistic ability. He's absorbing everything around him and putting it into his art, and his excellent work reflects his self-discipline and practice. He could easily use his gift to launch himself into a successful business that would be appropriate to his age—painting murals, doing Web site graphics, drawing dealer ads on the windshields of the vehicles for sale in car lots—and the business skills he learns now would give him enormous confidence and prepare him well for an adult career that combines his talents with the means to earn a good living.

But Mr. Mercado can't see that. He doesn't understand that Paul is very lucky in knowing at a young age exactly what he wants to do. Neither does he see that through his art, Paul has already begun to develop traits that will help him succeed—qualities such as concentration and attention to detail. And because he is so uncomfortable with what he finds unfamiliar, he has no appreciation for the joy Paul gets from exercising his talents, pleasure that would be a prime motivator for him throughout his working life.

He should be applauding his efforts but is instead setting him up for frustration and failure. For starters, Paul is already out the $250 I wanted to pay him for his mural, not to mention the dozens of referrals I would have given him!

Little Business Now, Big Business Later

You may now agree that Mr. Mercado should let Paul paint my sons' bedroom. But you may still find it hard to believe that there is a real connection between work done by young people—like mowing lawns, washing cars, or in Paul's case, painting a mural—and the "real," grown-up world of successful entrepreneurship and millionaire status. *It's all very good to earn a little pocket money*, you think, *but for most kids these odd jobs are hardly a recipe for a life's work.*

But these jobs are actually the *best* recipe for life's work. When a child, no matter how young, is creating jobs for himself, he is doing much more than making some extra money to buy an iPod—he's developing self-reliance and confidence in his own ability, and he's discovering that the world really is filled with opportunity.

He is also learning practical business skills. If your son has a car-washing business, he must market his product—should he slip flyers under neighbors' doors, approach people personally, look for the dirtiest cars on the block? He must price his product—what is the charge for a regular car wash? how much can he charge if he does more detail work, like washing tires? He must become adept at customer relations—how can he get referrals? what should he do if someone complains about the job he did?

In fact, what he is doing in your driveway is what most adults do every day at their offices, and he's learning all this when he's fourteen years old. Further, instead of being a cog in someone else's machine, he's in charge of the whole show. He can arrange his work schedule around his baseball games. He can expand his business to another neighborhood. He can hire his siblings and friends to work for him. He can politely refuse to wash Mr. Winter's car because the man doesn't pay on time. He can earn as much money as he's willing to work for. What's not to love about this extraordinary learning-and-earning process?

Let's be honest. Wouldn't you like to have a job like that?

So let us begin to think of your children in new ways. What talents do they have that make them unique? If you encourage them, what kinds of businesses could they start, using their innate talents?

Maybe your son likes to fiddle with the computer or your daughter has a tendency to burst into song like a Broadway star at a moment's notice. You might not have paid attention to these traits—you may even rue them if, for instance, your son, without telling you, moved your e-mail account from America Online to Yahoo because he thinks it is better—but these individualized gifts could be the seeds of a business opportunity for your children. Your son's interest in the computer indicates curiosity and technological ability that, if harnessed to some business expertise, could earn him money right now!

When you take the time to really observe your children and teach them to celebrate and develop their enthusiasms, you are giving them the gift of believing in themselves and making it pay!

Entrepreneurial Education

Ready and eager to help your child? Let's change the way you think about money and work so that you can be one in the growing number of parents who guide their children to entrepreneurial success.

Take the Fear Out of Money

How do you talk to your child about money? Raise your hand if you've ever said one of the following: "Money doesn't grow on trees." "Do I *look* like an ATM machine?" "I don't care what your friend Campbell has—we can't afford it."

It's very important to teach your child to respect money. But teaching her to respect it is different from teaching her to fear it. When you constantly put the word *don't* in conversations about money—as in *"Don't* waste money," *"Don't* spend too much," or *"Don't* assume there's more where that came from"—you are spreading fear.

Take the threats out of your references to money. Money will always be there when your child needs it, *if* she's willing to work, is sensible, and absorbs the business principles you teach her. That's the message you want to convey, because, believe me, it's true.

Share the Good News About Work

You obviously know if you like or hate your job. But guess what? So does your child.

Even if you never talk about your work, he sees how unhappy you are when you drag yourself out the door in the morning and when you crawl back in at night. He hears you complain about your boss, your coworkers, and your pay. He also notes that you have a spring in your step when you come in the door after a good day at work or when you share a funny story about something that happened in the office. Whether you like it or not, you and your spouse are the closest connections he has to the world of work. So it's important to be as positive as you can about work and the fact that making money can be fun! While some truly loathe their jobs and really can't say anything good about how they spend their days, there are many parents who like what they do but don't share their joy with their children because they're just too tired at the end of the day or wrongly think their children won't be interested in their workday details.

But say you're a real-estate agent who sized up a new client, knew exactly which house she would like, showed it to her, and already got an offer to buy it. Don't you think your daughter would like to know how you figured out from the way the client dressed, the town she was moving from, and how she talked about her garden that she would like an older, colonial house rather than a modern ranch with a beautiful swimming pool? You bet she would! And she'll be equally interested when you explain to her that you'll earn a commission on the sale, what percentage the commission is, and how to calculate it based on the house's selling price. She'll be excited for you when you tell her that if the sale goes through, you'll take the family out to dinner at her favorite restaurant or begin saving for a new car or a family vacation. She will have learned from you that work can be stimulating and that it's OK to dream of the financial rewards you can realize from it.

Step Out of Your Grown-up Suit

If you've been brought up with the myths I described earlier and have the overly cautious attitudes about money that your own parents may have drummed into you, it might be difficult to let go of old ways of thinking.

But you can do it for your children's sake!

Close your eyes and think about your own childhood. When you were young, it was Saturday morning, and you had the day ahead of you, what did you most like to do? Watch cartoons? Ride your bike? Play your electric guitar? Visit the library? Go shopping with your friends? Climb a huge tree in the backyard? Whatever you liked to do was probably something you were good at and was an indication of where your gifts lay.

Your own parents may not have encouraged you to pursue your interests, or if they did, they probably didn't think of them as anything more than childhood fantasies that would fade as you grew up. They may have even discouraged you from pursuing any of your interests with any passion, because they didn't want you to lose sight of "real world" concerns, such as school and work. With the best of intentions, they may have kept you from working at goals that would have led you to jobs more enjoyable for you than what you now do for a living.

But you have the opportunity to do just the opposite with your own kids. No matter their ages, from six to sixteen, your own children's interests and behavior are clues to their talents, and by learning how to identify their gifts and helping them match their abilities to job opportunities, you are starting them on the road to satisfying and productive futures.

It's not easy to shed a lifetime of don'ts for a new world of "go-for-it," but if you've picked up this book, you're ready to try, and I'm here to help you, just as I've helped many, many parents in my years of working with young entrepreneurs. And once you do trade in those old-school fears and limitations for a millionaire mindset, you'll be ready to do the next important thing on the road to helping your child be a millionaire—become his mentor.

TWO

Mentor Magic

SET THE STAGE FOR CHANGE

When I was growing up in Alaska, my father took me, one Saturday morning a month, to our local Denny's, where he would order a cup of coffee, I would get a hot chocolate, and we would sit and talk about our ideas. We both love cars, and he would say something like, "I have a crazy idea for a car with a driver's seat in the back." Then we would both start drawing on napkins and discussing how it would be built.

Obviously there wasn't a big market for cars with a driver's seat in the back (there are already enough backseat drivers in the world!), but that wasn't why my dad invited me to breakfast at Denny's. The real aim of our meetings, I now realize, was to teach me how to dream and to give me the confidence to believe that I could realize those dreams. My father knew how important that was.

He was my first and best mentor. And I want to help you do for your children what my father did for me. Every young entrepreneur needs a mentor to guide him or her on the road to success.

Mentor Basics

A successful mentor provides two things to a young entrepreneur: inspiration and practical help. Even if you've never made a dime on an entrepreneurial idea, you can still be a great mentor to your children, primarily because you love them and want to see them succeed. Please don't underestimate yourself.

If you have some level of business success yourself, that's great. Are you a salesperson who loves your work and knows how to close a deal? A small business owner who makes a good living? An at-home mother who runs the annual and very successful fund-raiser at your daughter's school? Then you already have entrepreneurial skills to pass along to your child.

But even if the whole concept of being an entrepreneur seems foreign, or even scary, to you, you'll be happily surprised at how easy it is for your children to understand and embrace the concepts you teach them. Most children take to being entrepreneurs like ducks take to water.

If you really feel uncomfortable mentoring your child, though, that's fine. Find a mentor for her—your sister who turned an at-home catering business into a thriving restaurant, or the neighbor who ran a computer-repair shop out of his garage and used the profits to rent an office that now employs a dozen computer technicians who repair most of the computers in town.

It's very important, though, that another mentor be as enthusiastic and committed to your child's future as you are. Belief in a child and in her abilities is key to successful mentoring. A good mentor takes the time to encourage a child to think creatively about her interests and talents and help her brainstorm about all sorts of job possibilities. She will learn that while not every idea is a winner, every idea leads to another and to another, until eventually she finds one that works for her. Tarzan swung from tree to tree to get to his destination. Each little idea or experience your child has is part of her journey.

So if you're ready to mentor, let's go!

Entrepreneurial Thinking

How many times have you heard an adult say to a child, "Enjoy being a kid now, because someday you'll be stuck like me, working day in, day out, *blah, blah, blah*"? Maybe (gulp) you have even said it yourself. Well, those days are over!

Now you understand that there is another way to spend a working life and are ready to embrace these new ideas for your child's sake. In your conversations with him, you must banish the idea of work as a separate box that you step into every day and count the hours until you can step out again. Instead, share with your child, if you can, the positive aspects of your own job and the rewards you get, both financially and emotionally. This sets the stage to encourage him to think about his own future as an exciting adventure. Eventually, you will also sprinkle in stories of things that didn't go well and what you learned from those failures. But for now, let's be as upbeat as possible.

Your goal is to help your child understand that work is nothing more than exchanging talent for money. This will reduce his anxiety (and maybe yours!) about money and allow you both to concentrate on your son's unique abilities. When he sees that his future financial success lies in discovering and developing his innate talents, he has learned a valuable lesson and will be extremely motivated to succeed. It's like giving him a checkbook and the bank vault to go with it!

Following the steps to come will guide you to unleashing your child's creativity, the first stride toward creating a future millionaire.

Inspire Your Child

Inspiring your child is the truly rewarding and exciting part of teaching your child to become a millionaire. The time spent talking to her, over a hot chocolate at Denny's, as my dad did, or wherever you and your daughter might comfortably have some time alone, will be something you will treasure your whole life. This is when you find out what makes her tick—her interests, her dreams, what she's good at, what she doesn't like. You may think you already know your child—after all, you live under the same roof—but you will be astounded by what you discover in your time together as you begin to lead her to think and talk about herself.

Let Your Child Dream

Foxhunters shout, "Release the hounds!" when they are ready to begin their adventurous hunt. Well, I say to parents, "Release the magic!" Let your child's entrepreneurial adventure begin.

Encouraging a child's natural optimism—his sense that anything is possible if he believes in his own creativity and ideas—is the most important and satisfying component of mentoring. Later you will sit him down with a calculator and inject some necessary reality into his plans, but for now, just let the genie loose. Nurturing the entrepreneurial spirit that dwells in the hearts of most children requires encouraging them to dream.

Cheer your child on when his ideas begin to percolate, no matter how wildly impractical these ideas are. If your ten-year-old son wants to draw a cartoon strip for the local newspaper, why not? Help him think about topics that might interest readers; then talk about how he could pitch the idea to the editor. Suggest that he think about other ways to make money on the cartoons, such as making greeting cards with cartoon characters that he could sell at school.

Or say your daughter loves playing with dolls and wants to buy more. Take her to your local hobby/craft store to buy doll parts that can be assembled and sold to her friends. What about clothes for the dolls? Does she like to sew? Maybe you could cover the cost for her to take a sewing class.

Many parents are enchanted by this aspect of mentoring. I'm delighted when one of my children opens up and talks to me about what he or she likes to do. No matter how fanciful it seems, I love the process of steering him or her toward a business opportunity that both excites him or her and makes financial sense.

Other parents are not so enthusiastic about these discussions because they seem so impractical and take so much time. How much money is your daughter really going to make selling chocolate chip cookies to friends and neighbors, and what is your kitchen going to look like?

But without taking the first step of dreaming and talking about what she likes to do and is good at, your child will never become a successful entrepreneur. Practically speaking, letting your daughter mess up your kitchen to make cookies when she's nine means she won't be hanging around the kitchen when she's nineteen, because she will be earning enough money to have her own kitchen.

Remember Santa Claus

For those parents who find it hard to understand the importance and pleasure of dreaming, I remind them of Santa Claus.

I *don't* mean you should ask him to get your son a job.

I mean that you should remember, if you celebrate Christmas, how much your children believe in Santa Claus when they are young and how much you encourage their belief.

Do they write letters to Santa that you take to the post office? Do you put out cookies and milk for Santa, which you gobble down at some point during the long night while you're putting together a dollhouse? Do you go down to the living room first and yell up to the kids, "Wow! I can't believe what Santa brought!" while they squeal in anguished anticipation at the top of the stairs?

What is that if not dream thinking? And don't you enjoy doing it?

If parents allow their children to pursue business opportunities with the same fervor and imagination that they themselves expend to create the magic of Santa Claus, they're on the right track as mentors.

Step Back to Go Forward

All the wishing in the world doesn't make dreams come true without planning and hard work, however, so while you're encouraging your daughter to share her ideas and hopes, you must also begin to guide her in the practical ways she can achieve financial success. Doing this, for many parents, means that they must take a few steps backward to set up a new dynamic for learning-to-earn.

Give Your Child the "Gift of Want"

On a plane trip about ten years ago, I sat next to an elderly woman, and we began to talk about our families, her three daughters, my then two children. Almost idly, to make conversation, I asked her what she thought was the most important thing a parent could do when raising a child.

She paused for a moment and told me she would think about it and tell me later.

I was surprised by how seriously she took my question, and even more so when she tapped me on the elbow later in the flight and said, "The greatest gift you can give to your child is the gift of want."

I was startled, because she seemed to be reading my mind. At the time, I was just beginning to make a very good living with my business. My wife and I, who had both grown up without much money, took great pleasure in giving our children everything we'd never had, and the result was that we were spoiling them to death.

Her advice brought home to me the memory of my own childhood and the pleasure I'd taken in wanting something and figuring out a way to get it. My situation had been different, because there was no alternative for me, but it also gave me the confidence and ability I've used throughout my life to create and succeed in business.

And now, here I was, through a combination of love and self-indulgence, denying my children the benefits of the very lessons that had been my reason for success. Giving them everything they could possibly want, and more, was no gift. All they could learn from our overgenerosity was to ask for *more* and appreciate what they had *less*.

I'm not alone in enjoying being able to indulge my children. It brings a parent great pleasure to give his child what he wants. But for those of us who have the means to do this, mentoring a young entrepreneur means *not* showering him or her with gifts. The "gift of want," as my wise fellow flier put it, will teach your child that he can be the architect of his own future and doesn't need to rely on others to get what he wants.

Some of you may be reading this and saying, "Give me a break. My kids already have the 'gift of want,' but it's no gift. I only wish I could give them the things they'd like."

Having a tight family budget would seem to make the gift of want a slam dunk in your family. But just as parents with ample means must exercise self-restraint in withholding presents from their children, so must parents with little disposable income be careful not to paint too desolate a picture about their lack of money. When your child asks for something, it may be tempting to forcefully remind him that you cannot indulge him when you have bills to pay or to apologize for not being able to give him what he wants. Resist this impulse! You want your child to feel the freedom to create his own business success, not be so discouraged by your own money problems that he doesn't even try. When I was growing up, there was no extra money for any extravagances, but instead of bludgeoning my brother and me with dire threats about our family's finances, my parents encouraged us to figure out a way to make money for ourselves. And we did. They turned lemons into lemonade. And you can do this as well, no matter how much money you have.

The gift of want needs to be taught to all children regardless of a family's financial circumstances. Without this tool, your efforts to teach your child how to become a millionaire are almost certainly doomed to failure. I cannot emphasize this enough—you *have* to free your child to want something very badly in order for him to become a successful entrepreneur and to have the hope that he can succeed. If you don't create an environment where your son is encouraged, even forced, to figure out a way to pay for what he wants, he won't "learn to earn."

So when you feel the urge to splurge on your child or, conversely, to lecture him when he asks you to buy him something you can't afford, hold back. Almost always, both you and your child will be better off for your restraint.

Stop the Allowance

The first and best way to teach your child the gift of want is to stop giving her an allowance, one of the most wrongheaded concepts that has ever been sold to well-meaning parents.

Allowances are a terrible disservice to your child, teaching her to be on the dole instead of earning her own money. Giving your daughter an allowance is like giving her a cookie instead of teaching her how to bake cookies for herself.

Why should you pay your child for being a productive member of the household? Does she pay you to make her dinner, or tip you when you do the laundry? Of course not, so neither should she get money for doing her fair share of the jobs that are a daily and necessary part of running a home.

Just as misguided is the idea that handing out an allowance with no strings attached teaches your child how to manage her own money. Hogwash. The only thing it teaches her is to be totally dependent on you for income.

Children need to learn as soon as they are able that money is not a gift but is compensation for work done, and that earning their own money gives them the freedom to spend it any way they like. Helping them learn to earn, rather than just handing money over to them every week, is the first and biggest step you can take to empower them to become future millionaires.

If your child has not heard of allowances, congratulations! You get to start with a clean slate. You can introduce the concept of earning money without the burden of the allowance myth at the beginning of your new mentoring role with your child.

If you've been giving your son or daughter an allowance for some time, however, cutting off the money supply is going to be as popular as mud, so you will have to explain your reasons, and they have to be positive, not punitive.

I will guide you through this conversation in a later chapter, as it will be a crucial component of starting your child on his or her path to becoming a future millionaire.

Don't Cave In

Changing the way you handle money with your child is a big adjustment for both you and him, and you might be tempted, amid busy daily schedules and a shortage of time, to return to old habits. Some children will jump at the chance to become the next Bill Gates, but most children will need steady guidance in becoming future millionaires. And some of you will find that your kids are appalled by the idea of working! They will do everything they can to persuade you to abandon your new, foolhardy thinking and turn the money tap back on.

These children can be very persistent, and parents can get very tired of being badgered and find themselves thinking, *Oh, why not give them some money? I can afford it.*

But you really can't afford it if you want your child to become financially successful and independent. Your goal is to encourage his "want" and help him figure out a way to work so that he can buy what he wants by himself.

So please don't succumb to cries of financial anguish and accusations of cruel and unusual punishment. Nod and read on, knowing that your children will soon thank you for your attention and interest. Saying no to their wants now is saying yes to their entrepreneurial growth.

Give Your Message with a Smile

Throughout this whole book, I will remind you of how important it is to make this journey with your son or daughter an enjoyable adventure. Even when delivering unpopular news, such as the end of the allowance era, be positive and encouraging.

The more you applaud your child's efforts and let him or her know how very much you want to help, the more eagerly your

24

child will respond to your suggestions. The two of you will find tremendous satisfaction from working together, and the rewards you enjoy will be as much emotional as financial.

Let the Games Begin!

Once you've seen the value of teaching your child new learn-to-earn strategies, you're ready to embrace my program to help your son or daughter become a future millionaire. In the following chapters, I will give you a blueprint for transforming your financially dependent child into an engaged and enthusiastic young businessperson whose creativity and hard work earn him enough money to buy anything he wants.

This education has a number of steps: identifying your child's business strengths; preparing for a first meeting to introduce him to the learn-to-earn philosophy; working with him to select his first profit-making enterprise; teaching him business skills as he sets up his dream business; and, finally, watching him reap the rewards of his success! So . . . let's get started!

THREE

The Millionaire March

IDENTIFY YOUR CHILD'S BUSINESS TALENTS

WITH YOUR WHOLE NEW OUTLOOK ON WORK, MONEY, AND opportunity and your understanding that successful businesses can be pleasurable as well as profitable, you can start the exciting work of transferring this life-changing knowledge to your child.

The first step in this brave new world is for you and your spouse to do some homework on your child's behalf, which involves identifying the interests and talents that will be his ticket to prosperity. You already know his favorite meals and can name his best friends and the school subjects he likes—why not figure out what will make him a success at business?

Focusing on his talents and interests will enable you to help him discover them for himself and then translate those gifts into skills that will become his tools to create businesses and make money. You can teach him to learn to earn in the same way you have taught him to ride a bike, catch a fish, or cook breakfast. Further, you will be doing this at a young age, when it is easiest for children to take in new concepts and information, before life patterns are established.

Your work now will give him a dramatic (some would even say unfair!) advantage over his peers, as he will have had at least fifteen years of business experience when he reaches adulthood. And that experience that will guarantee his chances of earning a very good living.

The top 10 percent of the wealthiest Americans earn an average of $256,000 annually, according to the American Affluence Research Center, an Aventura, Florida, market research company. Yet according to the U.S. Congressional Budget Office, the average household income is below $44,000.

Wouldn't you like your child to be in the top 10 percent of wealthy Americans? Of course!

The very good news is that if you work now to help him recognize his talents and give him the confidence and practical advice to convert them into money and a possible career, he will be trained for financial success, earning enough to be in that top 10 percent. That's the job I'm here to help you with.

The Inner Entrepreneur

Successful entrepreneurs have learned to trust their instincts, know their strengths, and build on both to create high-earning businesses. You are going to help your child do the same by zeroing in on the traits that make her who she is. Her personality and interests will serve as a template for businesses that will best suit her.

I urge you and your spouse to do this together. Two heads are better than one in teasing out the important traits of your child, and, just as important, when you do this together and provide a united front, your child will be much more likely to move forward without friction. This is very much a family affair.

Note: if you are not mentoring your child yourself, then you and the mentor can work together on this important initial phase.

Describe Your Future Millionaire

When talking about your son or daughter, what adjectives do people use? What adjectives do *you* use? Noting these descriptions is your first task in service of your future millionaire.

You and your spouse/partner can sit down with a pencil and paper and write down all the adjectives that come to mind when thinking of your child. Note every single one that you both have thought of yourselves and remember hearing others say about your child: kind, nosy, generous, angry, pretty, serious, lazy, popular, cute, insecure, quiet, loyal, needy, bookish, peppy, mean, easygoing, focused, happy, introspective, noisy, outdoorsy, nerdy, short-tempered, athletic, funny, handsome, arty, cooperative, conscientious, naive, adventurous, nervous—you name it. You should have a minimum of fifteen adjectives that describe all of the aspects of your child's personality, but please write down as many as you can think of. This is a very important exercise. Spend as much time on it as you can, as it serves as a blueprint for all your work with your future millionaire.

The list will give you insights you've probably never had about your son or daughter and make you wonder why you waited so long to find out about him or her! It's fascinating to learn so much about your child and know that you're going to use that knowledge to help your child toward an exciting and financially secure future.

Celebrate the Stubborn Child

When you look over your list, some of you will find adjectives that are often seen as negative, words like *stubborn, talkative,* or *bossy.* If you do, count your lucky stars! Those traits will be a big asset to your future millionaire.

Many personality traits are not admired in our get-along world—resistance to authority, seeming hyperactivity, or the opposite, "spaciness"—but these parts of a child's makeup are usually the very ones that signal his special talents. Your child may have been labeled this way by any number of well-meaning people, such as teachers, relatives, or doctors, and they may have persuaded you to think of these traits as "bad" and needing to be corrected. You yourself may even wish them away so that your child will act more like your neighbors' children, but please don't do this! These are your child's unique traits and must be nurtured if he is to become who he is meant to be, to succeed on his own terms. I'm not saying that you throw up your hands and condone all behavior regardless of consequences, but it is crucial that you recognize every aspect of your son or daughter's personality in a neutral and/or positive way and put your energy into helping your child put those qualities to constructive use. I've had to learn this lesson along with all parents, most recently with one of my sons, a very strong-minded four-year-old.

Last Easter Sunday our family was at church, our sons and daughter in Sunday school, my wife and I in the service. About halfway through, I felt a tap on my shoulder and turned to find one of the Sunday school teachers motioning me out.

It turned out that Trace had taken off his shoes and jacket and was refusing to put them back on.

"He said, 'I'm *not* going to put on my shoes and jacket, and that's the way it's going to be,'" the Sunday school teacher reported with just the slightest tone of disapproval and exasperation. Trace was not making her day.

At that moment, I very much wanted him to be like all the other kids in Sunday school who kept their clothes on, so that I could be a part of the adult Easter service and not have to worry about him. But as I followed the teacher back to the Sunday school room, I realized I had to put my money where my mouth was. Here was a child exhibiting the very trait of stubbornness that I always caution parents not to think of negatively. Clearly, I would have to tell Trace to put his shoes and jacket back on, but at the same time, I did not want to break his spirit. He is a child who does not go along with the crowd and, in fact, doesn't care at all what the crowd, or his teacher, thinks. While this is a terrible attribute in a classroom, when a teacher is trying to manage a dozen four-year-olds on sugar highs from early-morning Easter baskets, it is a really great gift to know what you want and insist on it against all odds.

So my challenge, like that of many parents, is to work with Trace to help him master his persistent nature to his benefit, and the best way to do that, given my experience, is to introduce him to some entrepreneurial business opportunities that will channel his determination and teach him some excellent money-making skills. In a later chapter, I will outline some good business outlets for young people like Trace, but for now I just want you to know that I'm in the trenches too!

The following are some adjectives commonly used to describe children who fall outside the normal ranges of behavior. Next to them I've named a few of the skills that children with these so-called negative traits often possess, skills that are terrific for business:

- Stubborn (persistence, self-confidence, nonconformity)

- Shy (contemplativeness, patience, ability to listen)

- Hyperactive (energy, impatience [to get things done], enthusiasm)

- Daydreamy (imaginativeness, creativity, originality)
- Show-offy (courage, "star" quality, public-speaking ability)
- Talkative (communicative, a "people person")
- Bossy (leadership, determination)

So banish those negative connotations when you're thinking of your own children, because as you can see, they're not bad at all. They're just the way some kids are, and those kids often turn out to be the most successful entrepreneurs.

If you are having trouble, think of some well-known entrepreneurs, from cookie queen Debbi Fields; to Steve Jobs of Apple Computers; to media mogul Ted Turner; to Larry Ellison, cofounder and CEO of the hugely successful database company Oracle. One or more of these adjectives can describe any one of them—your child may be in very good company!

Identify Your Child's Interests

After you've compiled a list of your son's or daughter's behavior traits, it's time for the next part of this job, which is to make a list of your kid's interests. What does he do outside of school?

Paying attention to this gives you further information important for business success, because how your child chooses to spend his leisure time is a clue to what kind of work will interest him. Skateboarders, computer geeks, and shopping junkies are all doing things they like, and there are business models that can accommodate all of these pastimes.

A person's hobbies and interests are also usually things he is good at, another reason to pay close attention to them, because if a child's gifts are properly channeled, the sky's the limit on what he can achieve. Google cofounder Larry Page was six years old when he first discovered his passion for computers, and his father, a computer science professor, encouraged his interest. George Parker was, with his brother, an avid game player when he was young. Does the name Parker Brothers ring a bell?

Make no mistake. When your child sees his interests as a career path rather than as just a pleasant way to spend time, he will have learned the invaluable lesson that successful entrepreneurs have known forever: "Do what you like and make it pay!"

What your son or daughter does also highlights what he or she *doesn't* like to do. A reader might not be a social schmoozer, while someone who spends all his time on the telephone would hate being isolated from his peers. Someone who likes computer games wouldn't be happy doing something physical outdoors. Being aware of this adds to the information you can use to plant seeds of success that will guide your child to future fulfillment.

So write everything down. Some kids are very busy with all sorts of hobbies, but most kids have two or three things they do most often in their free time. Note everything you see, no matter what age your child is, from playing with toy trucks to playing organized sports. Obsessing about cars; being outdoors or indoors most of the time; helping you cook; reading; playing computer games or e-mailing friends; building things; drawing; and listening to music are all activities that indicate interests that can come into play when you and your child are figuring out possible money-earning business ventures.

Please make sure you write this list with your spouse, because depending on your differing schedules, you most likely see your child at different parts of the day and evening and thus have differing but equally important information to create a complete picture of what your child likes to do. Also, each of you has individual insights about your child that can only enrich your work with him or her.

Combined with your list of descriptive adjectives, you now have a good sense of what your youngster is like and what drives him or her. The work you've done will give you tremendous insight about what opportunities your child could successfully pursue.

The Right Business

Now it's time to put on your thinking cap and match your child's personality and interests to some job possibilities.

Begin to think of enterprises that might be suitable for your son or daughter, depending on his or her personality, interests, age, and schedule. Aim for business opportunities that make the best use of the traits and interests you identified. If every single working person did this, our world would be a very happy place!

Your physically active son might loathe a job watering house-plants for a vacationing neighbor but would love rounding up neighborhood boys for an after-school playgroup once a week.

An anxious child needs self-confidence and maybe time to hang out with Mom and Dad, so weeding in the garden with you while you supply both encouragement and money for a job well done would be a good fit for her.

At the same time that you're thinking about your son's or daughter's talents, think about the business opportunities in your neighborhood. Are there older people who might appreciate some-one to do chores around the house or run errands? Is the block filled with small children who need to be entertained while their mothers cook dinner? What about lawn work, car washing, waiting for deliveries—these are all possible business ventures for your son or daughter, depending on his or her interests, age, and amount of free time.

Once you start, you will be surprised at what ideas will surface. To further help, I've outlined some terrific kid-friendly businesses in later chapters that you can adapt to your own child and community.

By doing this ahead of time, you will have some promising businesses in mind before you sit down and talk to your child, and you can grab her interest right away. Once excited by your ideas, your child will begin to think of her own as well, and your first meeting will go very smoothly. Your aim is to help your youngster start a business and earn money as quickly as possible so that she will see the benefits of the learn-to-earn philosophy. Kids are not long-range planners—if they can start a small business and earn enough to go to Kmart and buy whatever they want, they will think your plan is the greatest. Later they will, on their own, make the transition from instant gratification to a more mature outlook on saving and spending, but in the short term, *money talks.*

Loose Lips Sink Ships

Once you've completed these exercises and have some intriguing job ideas for your child, you're going to be so excited about the possibilities for her that you'll want to burst into the room and shout, "Have I got a future for you!" If you do this, I will find out where you live, come to your house, and hit you over the head with a large, blunt instrument.

DO NOT SPEAK TO YOUR CHILD NOW.

This is the most important warning of this chapter, because heeding it will make the difference between whether this program works or is a complete disaster.

What you are doing right now is setting the stage for your child's entire life. This is the beginning of a journey for your future millionaire, the first step in a new, radical way of thinking about your child's future. (It shouldn't *be* radical—it should be the norm, but that's another story.) You are teaching your youngster to believe in herself—to use her natural gifts to create work for herself and to understand that what she is doing now can be done *throughout* her life to achieve a success beyond her (and your) wildest dreams.

Your job as a parent is to shape a learn-to-earn blueprint and then gently guide your child to think that all the ideas are his or hers. If you do this, your son or daughter will get to the point where most of the ideas and decisions *are* his or hers, which is just what you want. But it is absolutely imperative that you don't tip your hand early and give any indication that you've already figured out what he or she would be good at and that you know just how to get there. If you do this, you will rob your child of the great and necessary gift of life—being in control of his or her own destiny. Your son must have the opportunity to discover himself by himself, your daughter to realize her gifts and how she can use them to get what she wants. Then your child will become the independent, confident man or woman you hope for. And, boy, will your grown child thank you for it.

Business Fundamentals

Now that you've got a good idea of your future millionaire's abilities and interests, you can concentrate more specifically on the types of businesses that you will suggest or, better yet, let him or her suggest to you.

Our next task is to make sure these opportunities meet certain practical criteria so that when your son or daughter at last launches a business, he or she will have smooth sailing. In the next chapter, we will outline these considerations to help you choose the best and most profitable enterprises for your child.

FOUR

Business Building Blocks

PAVE THE PATH FOR SUCCESS

WE'RE GETTING CLOSE! CONSIDER THIS CHAPTER A CHECKLIST for success, because if you make sure the business ideas that you suggest to your future millionaire are practical, workable, and engaging, your child will be able to jump with both feet into an exciting and profitable enterprise.

Following are the fundamentals to consider when selecting possible business ventures for your young entrepreneur.

Safety

Whatever your child does must be safe. Small children are naive and can be easily conned; even older children can be vulnerable to those with bad intentions. Logic and good judgment will guide you to steering a young child away from door-to-door sales to strangers or from business locations unsuitable for your child. Both of you should be very comfortable that when your youngster is at work, he or she is not in harm's way.

Economic Feasibility

Most businesses require at least a little start-up money, and chances are that money will come from you. If your daughter is interested in making doll clothes, you'll be out the money for fabric and sewing notions. If she wants to shovel snow, she needs a shovel. So have some realistic financial guidelines in mind before you talk to her about possible businesses. If $25 is all you can afford to launch your entrepreneur's business, steer her to business opportunities that meet that criteria. Many businesses can be started for very little money, and by setting practical parameters for your own budget, you can be positive and encouraging to your child without worrying about money.

Logistics

My first business venture was a curb-painting business with my brother. We persuaded homeowners in our housing development, where all the houses looked alike, to pay us to paint their house numbers on the curb to help visitors—and pizza deliverers!—find their homes. It was a great business concept—except that we lived in Alaska, where it snowed about eight months of the year, hiding the curbs and considerably curbing (so to speak) our business opportunities.

When setting up a business plan, you need to address the seasonal and physical aspects of an enterprise as well as the resources available to make it successful. If your ninety-pound daughter wants to sell watermelons, ask her if she can lift a lot of four-pound watermelons off a truck. Her answer will likely steer her to another idea. A cookie-baking business needs a stove, so figure out when your young baker can use your kitchen without driving the rest of the family crazy.

Always keep these discussions upbeat, however. Your goal is to go along with your child's plans as much as possible while at the same doing everything you can to ensure that he or she will both succeed and learn about business along the way. I'm sure my father was very aware of the pitfalls of my brother's and my curb-painting business, but he helped us do everything from buying the paint to telling the neighbors about our business. We thought we were pretty smart when we earned enough money to buy the bikes we wanted, but we also learned a good lesson in business planning—consider the weather when setting up an outdoor business!

Legal Requirements

Each state has different requirements regarding children and business, but generally, minors cannot enter into business contracts or get lines of credit without an adult cosigning a legal document. My Web site, YoungBucks.biz, outlines these requirements state by state, but you can also call the nearest office of your state government to find out the legal regulations for children who have businesses.

Gear Your Pitch by Age

Children's responses to entrepreneurial ideas will differ dramatically according to their ages. I've identified four basic age categories and will describe in a general way what you can expect when you talk to a child of any age about business. Knowing ahead of time how your six-year-old might react when you suggest picking up the pinecones in the front yard or what your fourteen-year-old is going to say to the idea of a dog-walking business, will help you present your ideas with the best chances for success. The younger your child, the easier it will be to introduce new ideas, but even teenagers can be successfully persuaded that they can become future millionaires.

Ages 5 and Under

These children for the most part haven't entered the school system and still truly live in a magical world—think Santa Claus, the Easter Bunny, and the Tooth Fairy. They are untouched by flawed philosophies (with the exception of any incorrect teachings in *your* house!). So, although very young, they are the most teachable and the most willing to believe that *all* things are possible.

You can assign these children simple jobs that can be mastered easily and quickly, pay them immediately, and let them spend the money equally fast. Children this age need instant gratification, so give it to them! Don't worry about spoiling them—they will naturally learn to exercise more restraint as they get older. This way they will be ahead of the curve at a very early age, able to think of themselves as successful entrepreneurs even if they have no idea what the word *entrepreneur* means.

Ages 6 to 10

The children in this age group are prime candidates for the introduction of learn-to-earn concepts. They have the belief systems of the younger kids but the attention span and drive of older children. They also are very fixed on strong "wants" at this stage, a big plus when motivating them. They are eager and believe *most* things are possible.

Your approach with these kids can be more sophisticated. They will participate in matching a job to their interests, can grasp the simple mathematics of business, and can understand the importance of marketing. It is pure pleasure working with this age group, as they are very happy to spend time with you, enjoy brainstorming, and love earning money and buying what they want.

Ages 11 to 14

This is the most challenging age group, because they are beginning to grow up and away from you and so are less willing to buy into the plans you suggest. (Another reason to start your future millionaire on the path to success as early as you can!) They are beginning to think that they're smarter than their parents, yet they're not so sure how smart they themselves are, which often makes for insecurity and rebelliousness. They are increasingly absorbed in their peers and don't want to look stupid or be different. It also doesn't help that their hormones are beginning to kick in, affecting their moods and focus.

Further, preteens and early teens can be, or at least pretend to be, very cynical. They believe *very few* things are possible, so persuading them of their own strengths and ability to succeed is tougher. But if you know all this ahead of time, you can tailor your talk to boost their self-esteem, remember to keep your cool when they challenge you, and have some really good job ideas ready so that they will become intrigued in spite of themselves.

As difficult as this age group is to work with, it can also be the most rewarding, because a successful business experience at this stage of a child's development can have the greatest impact of any of the four age groups. When a pre- or early teen creates a successful job for himself, his self-confidence soars along with his bank account, and he often gets a valuable new sense of himself.

Ages 15 to 18

Unlike the previous group, kids in their mid to upper teens believe *many* things are possible, and the learn-to-earn philosophy with a young person this age can bring fast results. They are *mini-adults* and, unlike the previous age group, are less affected by peer pressure and are more mature and focused. They have started asking themselves big-life questions about their educations, careers, and lifestyles and are also more aware of the real costs of living and the tremendous, ongoing need for money.

At the same time, kids of this age are more "want" driven, which is a big plus for you. If, for instance, your teenage daughter wants a car and you haven't caved in and bought her one, this "want" alone could launch a very successful beginning to teaching her to be a future millionaire.

To stimulate young people this age to start thinking about using their gifts to make money, treat them like the young adults they're becoming. No more "kiddie" businesses here. Teens will be interested in doing something more meaningful and profitable.

If a child this age was introduced to learn-to-earn techniques while still young, future millionaire habits will be firmly rooted, and your teen will have accumulated some wealth. A child who is just beginning at this age, however, can still progress at a very, very fast rate, because she will be motivated to earn money, receptive to your ideas, willing to work hard, and more apt to stick to projects than younger children.

Personal Basics

More important than the business fundamentals just discussed is the answer to this question: is your future millionaire happy? He who dies with the most toys does not win. But he who dies with the most *joys* does win. That's my ultimate objective here—to bring greater joy into the life of your child, both now and later, when he or she is an adult. Please keep this goal in mind at all times when mentoring your child through this experience. It's OK to have fun along the way!

Make Work Exciting

It's extremely important that your child be very excited about whatever business he chooses. If your son is not really interested, it's never going to fly. So when you talk to your child, listen carefully to his responses and be very encouraging of any ideas that you hear.

This can be a tricky time for good mentors. You really want your child to start the business that *you* thought of, a neighborhood computer-tech venture. He's already the go-to person in your household for computer questions. Furthermore, there are no start-up costs, you have a long list of customers in mind, and you know he could make quite a bit of money. The only drawback is that he's not so excited about your idea. He wants to draw cartoon characters, print them on postcards, and sell them at school and at a local fair in a few weeks.

Your first inclination is to discourage his cockamamie idea— the computer-tech business is far sounder in every way, and he could earn *lots* of cash. But the better move is to drop your plan, endorse his, and help him turn it into a successful venture, not because cartooning is a better business, but simply because that's what your son wants to do.

Wait a minute, here! Wasn't *I* the one who asked you to spend all that time identifying the traits that would make your son successful in different businesses so you could help him pick the *best* business for his talents? (Which, by the way, did not include drawing evil-looking robots!) Well, yes, but I have an ulterior motive. Your son's eagerness to start a cartoon business will serve him (and you) well as you move to your next task for him, which is to teach him the tools to set up his business. If he goes along reluctantly with your idea of being a computer tech, however, he is already a step behind other entrepreneurs in having a little less enthusiasm, a little less ambition, a little less desire to succeed. He is also more likely to quit before he's made much money.

But if you support his favorite idea, rather than your own, you're doing two important things.

First, you are keeping him engaged and eager to learn how to formulate and implement a good business plan. These skills are what will make your son a future millionaire, no matter what business he undertakes.

Second, you are giving him the gift of thinking with his heart as well as his mind. Successful entrepreneurs are those who have been empowered to follow their dreams and make them work. By supporting your son in this way, you are encouraging him to believe in himself and trust his own instincts. That kind of self-confidence pays off in a big way, emotionally and financially.

So relax, accept his decision, and help him figure out how to make his cartooning business work. A month from now, he might decide he can't make enough money selling his cards and may appear at the breakfast table one morning asking you about the computer-tech business. Or his card business might take off, thanks to his hard work and creativity, and you can help him expand his business.

Keep Business in Balance

You are obviously very excited about the new enterprise your child is going to start, but it pays to remember that she is still in school and still loves to play sports or hang out with her friends. In other words, she's still a child, so her business shouldn't overtake the rest of her life.

Keeping a business "kid-sized" can be a challenge for a mentor who sees endless opportunity in a business idea—ways to increase profits, expand the customer base, and so on. But it's crucial to let your future millionaire call the shots on how much time she wants to spend working. If your thirteen-year-old daughter spends most Saturdays cleaning pools and can never hang out with her friends, she's going to lost interest in her work and burn out, no matter how much money's she's making! Much better for her future business career is to encourage her to balance work and play.

Don't we all wish for that balance in our own lives? Teaching your child this important concept now is a great gift to him or her.

Money Isn't Everything

Despite what you've told your son or daughter, remember that this first job is not about the money. It's OK for your child to think that he is only in business to earn some cash, but your priority at this early stage is to help him discover the pleasure of creating something of his own, learn some basic business concepts, and gain confidence in personal skills.

It's wonderful when your child makes money on his first business, which is inevitable, thanks to your good mentoring. But at the same time you're congratulating your son on profits earned, take time to explain to him all the business skills he is acquiring. Doing so will boost your future millionaire's self-confidence and keep him moving forward to the next opportunity, the next chance to put his talents to good use. Believe me, the money will follow.

Fun

Once you've addressed the nuts and bolts I've just described, the biggest priority for this first business venture is fun, fun, fun! I don't say this lightly. A child *has* to enjoy this first outing, or you will lose him, so let this adventure unfold at *your child's* pace. Guide your little entrepreneur gently, and don't push too hard.

Time to Talk to the Future Millionaire

When you've absorbed the principles in this chapter, identified your child's business strengths, and put together some ideas for possible businesses in which the child can succeed, you're ready to meet with your future millionaire.

The next chapter walks you through this all-important meeting so that when you sit down and talk with your future millionaire, everything will flow easily. This will be a gradual process, so take your time with your child. You will enjoy the ride, your child will reap the benefits for a lifetime, and your future grandchildren will be born into happy and financially secure families.

FIVE

The First Meeting

LIGHT THE LEARN-TO-EARN FIRE

Now is when the fun begins—introducing your future millionaire to your learn-to-earn program! You are about to take a financially dependent young person whose only connection to money is probably her allowance and teach her the basics of entrepreneurial thinking. As you work together, she will race ahead of her peers in understanding how to use her interests, talents, and personality to make money, she will blossom with self-confidence, and the two of you will enjoy this success together. What's not to like?

Because this first meeting is so important to your young entrepreneur, I'd like to walk you through the preparation for the meeting and give you some tips on how to engage your son or daughter in your ideas. You can take advantage of my experience by combining it with your own knowledge and good instincts, and your future millionaire will be off and running!

The Pitch

Talking to your child is really no different from preparing for a business meeting. You are going to make a sale—persuading your son to buy into your new, exciting way of thinking about money—and the best way to do this is to think like the buyer, anticipating his questions, concerns, and fears, and then have solid, reassuring answers for them all.

First, remember that all of this will be very new to your child. While you've been exploring exciting business opportunities he might enjoy, he has been operating on the old family system, maybe being told that money "doesn't grow on trees," perhaps begging you to buy him what he wants, possibly working at a simple job for extra cash. Whatever his attitudes toward money, he's in the dark ages compared to your new way of thinking.

So go slowly, pitching your ideas the same way you teach him to hit a baseball, by throwing the ball easily so that he has no trouble connecting bat to ball.

Second, keep the first meeting short. Give him time to ponder the notion that he's going to be his own breadwinner and you're going to help him, but resist the temptation to launch into all of your plans for him. He could easily be overwhelmed and then discouraged by all that's expected of him. Instead, focus on the destination, which is buying what he wants, and leave the details of the journey for later. There will be plenty of time to talk in future meetings.

Third, starting with this very first conversation, encourage his participation. Ask questions, and answer his questions with more questions, even though you already know the answers. Your goal is to open a dialogue, not lecture him. You want him to feel empowered, not overwhelmed. Think of yourself as the electric company for your house—you've laid the wires and done all the installation. But it's your son who will come home, flip the switch, and think he's the one who's turned on the lights!

Last, have fun, and look like it! Smile and nod as you talk and listen so that your son sees how much you're enjoying the wonderful opportunity of getting to know him, enjoying his company, and learning together.

The Right Time to Talk

The time for your first meeting with your son is when he's dying to buy something he can't afford—this "gift of want" I described earlier in chapter two.

Let's say that one day you pick up your eleven-year-old son after soccer practice and he tells you that his best friend, Alex, just got a cell phone. Alex now can call Spencer, another friend who also has a phone. And Ben too. It might be a good idea, he tells you, if he got one too.

Don't say anything right away, because this is the first time he has expressed this want, and you're not sure if he really wants a cell phone himself or is just reacting to his friend's purchase. So just nod and listen without making any promises.

A few days later he will again bring up the cell phone, perhaps embellishing his request by saying that it would be good for *you* if he had a cell phone so that you'd know exactly when to pick him up after practice. This is when you perk up your ears, because he's beginning to really, really want that cell phone.

Now is when you think about microwave popcorn.

I don't care what the package directions for microwave popcorn *say*—we all know that getting the corn popped without either burning it to a gummy, black blob or getting stuck with fistfuls of uncooked kernels is much more art than science. Forget setting the timer for two, three, or four minutes and walking away. You have to *listen* to the corn popping and wait for just the right lull between *pops* to open the door and retrieve the bag.

This is exactly what you have to do with your child—listen carefully to know just when you can introduce your learn-to-earn theory. You have to wait until his "want" has ripened to the plucking point so that he's primed for ideas on how he can earn the money to buy his cell phone. But you can't wait too long, or he will have given up hope and won't be receptive to your ideas. Getting the timing right is essential if you're going to succeed.

But who better to do this than you? You know your child well, and when you really pay attention to what he says and how he says it, you will be pleasantly surprised, because you'll know exactly when you can breach the subject.

When this moment does come, say something like, "That's an interesting idea. Why don't we talk about it?" The two of you can then set up a meeting. You should be alone with him—no siblings shouting, "Me too!" in the background—and also pick a time when you know you can both concentrate. This could be in the car together, after dinner one night, before bed, or on a quiet Saturday morning.

It's important to set a firm time, just like a business meeting. Doing so gives your child something to look forward to. He will know that you think it is important. A firm appointment also forces you to budget the time necessary to make it happen for your child.

The Magical First Meeting

Now it's finally time to sit down with your child and begin what will be a life-changing conversation. Ask him to tell you all about the cell phone—which one he wants, what features it has, how much it costs, and so on. Believe me, he's been talking about this with his friends, and he'll be bursting with information, because he's thinking, *Great! Mom's gonna buy me a cell phone!*

When he's done, you agree that a cell phone does sound like a good idea. He's old enough; it would be nice to be able to keep in touch; and so forth.

Right now is when the new journey begins.

Instead of saying, "Sure, we'll buy it for you," or "That could be your birthday present," as you may have done in the past, you're going to confess that you've done a lot of thinking about the cell phone, and it has made you realize that you've made some serious mistakes in teaching him about money.

If you've been giving him an allowance, this is when you say something like, "It's clear that a $5 allowance isn't anywhere near enough for you to buy a cell phone," and then go on to explain that an allowance isn't really realistic or helpful anyway. If he does some household chores in exchange for his allowance, you explain that it's hardly fair to pay him to do things that are part of living in a family—that you don't get paid for driving him to school every day. And you apologize for your wrongheaded thinking.

At this point, your child will be in shock. He launched into this conversation thinking he was minutes away from money to buy what he wanted and now finds out that not only is there no free cell phone on the horizon, but he's going to be out his allowance too!

But he really, really wants that cell phone, so you've still got his attention.

"So I was thinking," you say in a casual tone, "that maybe you could think about starting your own business and earn the money yourself."

Stop and wait for his answer, which will probably be the question, "How?"

You can explain that you've been thinking how good he is at something, like teaching his brother how to play computer games, or how carefully he organizes his Pokemon cards, and that you think he could use those talents in a few jobs that would earn him money. Name the jobs, and then ask him what he thinks.

Or if you think he might resist your ideas and need to feel more independent, you can say, "Why don't you think of a few things, and I will too. We can each make a list and talk about them."

Either way, you will be talking to him about money, encouraging him to think aloud about turning his talents and interests into income sources. Note: The jobs you suggest shouldn't be regular household chores, as maintaining a household is the unpaid responsibility of all the members of the family. Jobs around the house can be those that you would pay someone else to do—yard work and car washing, for instance, often fall into this category.

Congratulations! You've taken the first successful step in mentoring your future millionaire. He's sitting in front of you right now, his mind unlocked and abuzz with all sorts of new thoughts about himself and his abilities. This is true even if he's not saying much.

In fact, he very likely won't say too much. While some children jump right into this conversation and are ready to start a job right away, most take a little while to absorb all this new information. After all, this is as new to them as it very recently was to you.

So if your child looks blankly at you, don't be surprised or discouraged. Suggest that he take a while to think about what you've talked about and together set up your next meeting to zero in on the right job for him.

Momentum

By arranging another meeting to follow this first one, you're giving your child the opportunity to sort through the very new ideas you've presented to him. You're also helping him get started on a job as soon as possible. The more quickly he starts earning money, the faster he can buy his "want," which will prove to him that this plan of yours is a pretty good idea and will motivate him to earn more money.

Having another meeting on the calendar also helps you be a better mentor.

Your child is going to be thrilled when he realizes that you've been really thinking about his talents and abilities and believe that he can make money on his own. After your talk, his wheels will start turning, and he'll soon have his own ideas about jobs he thinks would be fun and profitable.

His enthusiasm will surprise you. In fact, when you are walking in the door from work or just sitting down to read the newspaper or going outside to garden, he will suddenly appear at your side to run another idea by you.

Even the most patient mentor can find this taxing, and your tendency might be to brush off your child, which is exactly what you don't want to do if you're trying to encourage his entrepreneurial instincts.

But if you have already set up another meeting, you can say, "Wow. That does sound interesting. Write it down right now so that we can discuss it at our meeting."

This way, both of you are still on board and enthusiastic about this new project. You're also reinforcing the new, organized way you and your child will interact.

Just make sure the second meeting happens quickly, preferably within a few days and certainly no more than a week later. Timing is all when launching a future millionaire!

So on to meeting number two, when you and your child will decide on a job and begin to set it up.

The First Business

Now's the time to zero in on a business opportunity! If your child is under five, choosing a business is up to you. He's too young to engage in a serious dialogue about his interests and abilities and doesn't really care anyway. He will be happy with anything you suggest as long as it suits his abilities and attention span and he can see the results quickly. Collecting all the plastic containers from the plants you bought and planted in the garden, getting paid, and going to the dollar store will make his day.

Any child over six, however, can participate fully in all the parts of selecting and creating a business, as long as you gear the information to his age level. For these children, this second meeting will start with your asking what ideas your son has come up with and then getting him to talk about them, teasing out details and encouraging his efforts. Don't worry if he shows up empty-handed, with no list; simply start with some of the ideas you have. Ask him what he thinks about them—this will begin the dialogue you're seeking. Ask your future millionaire lots of good questions, and carefully listen to his answers. He will soon become involved and very enthusiastic about business possibilities. Take notes as you talk to help you and your son narrow your choices and show him that you think his ideas are important enough to record.

Use the fundamentals in Chapter 4 to guide your young entrepreneur to a successful business. Does it interest him? Is there a need for the business, or can you create a need? (The mothers in the neighborhood might not know that they'd love to have someone take their kids for an hour before supper until your son sets up a playgroup.) Does he have the time and resources to launch the business? If he doesn't, how can you tailor the business so that it does suit his schedule?

So go to it, throwing out ideas, listening to your child's ideas, and discussing all these options, all the while making sure that you listen more than you talk, suggest more than you insist, and smile more than you frown (in fact, you shouldn't frown at all!). You will be surprised at how easily the ideas flow once you have uncorked your young entrepreneur's imagination, and you will be very pleased to find that you and your child will come to a good decision quite naturally. Before you know it, you will be saying, "That sounds great! Go for it, and I'll help you."

While occasionally it takes a third meeting to finally nail down the enterprise your child wants to start—an older child might need to do some additional research on a more sophisticated venture—most of you should be able to select a workable and exciting business at this meeting.

Sound the Trumpets!

Congratulations! The career of yet another future millionaire has begun, but this time the future millionaire is your own son or daughter.

By following my learn-to-earn program, you are beginning to teach your child to think in an exciting new way about earning money. Thanks to your encouragement and guidance, he has taken the first important step toward acting on his newfound knowledge. The skills you continue to teach him will all come from this first successful foray into the world of business. This is a very important day for both of you.

I also want to congratulate you on your own journey from old to new thinking about business. As you have mapped out a plan for your son, you very likely have thought a lot about how your own attitudes about money were shaped by your parents, and perhaps you feel ready to make some changes in your own life. I encourage you to do this as long as you keep your own dreams separate from your son's. He needs to follow his own dreams at his own pace; by keeping that always uppermost in your mind, you will guarantee his success.

Now, with a new business to begin, your son is off and running. It's time to walk you both through the nuts and bolts of setting up a business, just as they do at business school, only in less time and for less money.

SIX

Business Begins

START THE START-UP

Now it's time to put the pedal to the metal! You are about to introduce your daughter to the ABCs of business. Even if the closest you've ever gotten to a business plan is your monthly budget, you will be able to help her set up a successful enterprise by following the guidelines I give you. *Marketing, branding, inventory control,* and *net* and *gross profit* are not words that might slip off your daughter's tongue, or your own, but she will master them all as she sets up her business.

Be Prepared

Following are the steps that entrepreneurs take before starting a business, and the ones you and your daughter will take together as she starts her first venture. Each section is a learning moment for your child, a way to teach her life skills that will lead to her future success, so take your time and do it right—this is a marathon, not a 5K race.

Your inclination will be to use your own experience and maturity to help your daughter get started quickly, but resist the temptation. Don't overwhelm her with your own expertise, or she won't gain the confidence and skills to be successful on her own.

When you teach her to drive, you don't reach over and grab the wheel to show her how to turn (even though you'd like to!); you let her get the feel of the road and learn to do it herself so that she'll become a confident driver. It's no different when building skills for lifelong business success—*she* has to be the one in the driver's seat.

In this way she learns to trust her own instincts, which is absolutely key to thinking like a future millionaire. All successful businesspeople, all successful *people*, period, have learned to listen to their inner voices to guide their decision making, and children need to be able to trust their instincts as well. So always let your daughter take the lead by asking her what she thinks and leading her to the answers. Make her believe that most if not all of the good ideas are hers, and she will have the self-confidence of a future millionaire!

Bring On the Lemonade

For simplicity's sake, we will say that your daughter has decided to sell lemonade for her first venture. There are many more fun and profitable businesses for your child to launch, which are discussed in the following chapters, but everyone is familiar with a lemonade stand, and the mechanics of selling lemonade will serve as a template for any work she undertakes. If you had a lemonade stand when you were a child that consisted of putting up a card table in your driveway, you will find it very rewarding to see how much more success your daughter will have with the same business

when you teach her a more professional method of creating and
sustaining her enterprise.

Name It to Claim It: Branding

Naming the business is the first job for your young entrepreneur. And it's a lot of fun! Remember what joy your children had
naming your new puppy or kitten? Well, thinking up the perfect
name for her business is just as creative and exciting. Your daughter will feel very empowered when she realizes she can pick any
name she wants because it's her business. Choosing a good name
will also teach her some basic sales techniques—a name should
be easy to spell and remember (both for her and for her customers) and should entice customers to buy her product.

So encourage her to talk about what's unique about her lemonade. Will the lemonade be pink? Will it be freshly squeezed? Sally's
Yummy Pink Lemonade!

Also, a good idea when naming a product is to take a field trip
with your child to look at signage. Businesses do this all the time.
How do the words, colors, and artwork on signs effectively lure customers to their product? Ask your daughter to point out signs
she likes, and then ask her to explain why she likes them. Children
are very visual. You will be surprised at how savvy she will be about
good ways to advertise her product. Then let her design her own
posters, flyers, or e-mails, and make sure you applaud them, even if
you think you could do it better yourself.

Count the Cash: Pricing

A young person often has no idea how much things cost or
how much people will be willing to pay for anything. When my
six-year-old son was setting up his lemonade business and I asked
him what he thought he could charge for a glass, he said five

bucks! To teach your daughter about reasonable pricing, take her to the beverage section of the local deli and check out the cost of a Diet Coke, or look through your own refrigerator and point out the cost of the beverages you buy.

Talk about the service she will be offering her customers. This is an important concept. Explain to her that anyone can go to the grocery store and buy lemonade mix, but because she is willing to do all the work of preparing the lemonade—mixing it, getting cups and ice, and serving the lemonade—she is providing a service that a customer will be happy to pay for. All these services are worth money, and your daughter will soon understand that the more services she provides to a customer, which in business terms is called *adding value*, the more she can charge.

Later you can introduce her to more creative pricing. People love a bargain, and she could offer a discount for two glasses of lemonade or throw in a moist towelette or a cookie for an extra ten cents—there are endless ways to maximize profits, even at a lemonade stand.

Here I Am: Location, Location, Location!

The famous words about real estate are also true in the lemonade business, so talk to your daughter about where she wants to set up her stand. Discuss the benefits and drawbacks of various locations—in front of your house, down the street, at a store, in the local park.

Every business needs customers to buy its products, so steer your daughter to sites where people gather, which might be a nearby mall rather than your driveway at the end of a dead-end street. Also help her consider how to pick a location to attract the people most likely to *want* what she's selling. A bookstore like Barnes & Noble is found in upscale neighborhoods where people buy books—in New York City they are in Greenwich Village and the upper west side of Manhattan but not in Times Square, which attracts tourists more interested in sightseeing than in book-buying. So your daughter should think *thirsty*! Where are people dying for cold drinks—a local sports field, a construction site, a playground, a high-traffic tourist district?

Your daughter may have to get permission to set up her stand. A city park might require a permit; other locations may not allow private vendors. You could help out here by scouting some likely sites and omitting those where your daughter would get turned down. In fact, don't be shy about stacking the cards in her favor. Your goal is to help her succeed at this first business. If you know the manager of your local supermarket and see the shopping center there crowded on Saturday mornings, call him and get his permission for your daughter's stand, and then guide her to suggesting that location. Drive her there to talk to the manager, who has agreed to pretend that this is the first time he's heard this request.

After she talks to the manager, walk around outside the store with your daughter. Watch how many people come in and out of the store, and note the particulars: is one entrance more popular than another? do people stop and look at the plants for sale outside the store before going in or as they come out? Once you've made these observations, you can then help her choose the best place to put her table.

The next issue is the question of timing—when to set up the stand and for how long. Talk to her about the busiest times of day at the supermarket, and discuss how long she would like to sit at the stand. This will vary depending on the age of the child, but you can help her figure out reasonable "store hours" that will suit her schedule and stamina.

Hear Ye, Hear Ye: Marketing

Marketing is the single most important skill for future millionaires. It is where the rubber meets the road. Your daughter could have the best lemonade in town with the best name and even a great location, but if she doesn't spread the word about her delicious drink, she won't make the money she could.

Traditional marketing is familiar to us all—billboards, newspaper advertisements, posters taped to light poles or displayed at the local dry cleaner's—and your daughter can do any or all of those things. But she can also use her personal contacts. Her school friends would likely come to her stand if they knew when she was there, so maybe handing out flyers in school would be a good idea. She could hand out the same flyers to her Brownie troop, her parents' friends, and people at her church. She could also tape a flyer in the window of the family car so everyone in the store parking lot could find out about her lemonade stand.

At her stand, of course, she will put a big sign on her table, but maybe she could put other signs in the area around the shopping center, alerting people to her location. Could she pay her sister to help her by handing out flyers to shoppers going into the store? Little sis may feel very grown-up helping big sis launch a business.

The businesses that can market their products effectively are the ones that will succeed, so time spent helping your daughter take advantage of all possible marketing outlets will serve her well in this business and in future businesses. Let's make Sally's Yummy Pink Lemonade stand a big success!

Gather the Goods: Inventory

Buying the ingredients to make the lemonade is another learning moment. Go to the supermarket together and compare the prices of all the lemonade mixes to see which ones offer the best value in terms of price and ingredients. Look at the different sizes of cups for sale and discuss how much lemonade you want to sell per cup. If your child is old enough for simple math, bring along a calculator to help make comparisons.

Should you offer diet lemonade as well as regular lemonade? A lot of people watch their weight or are on sugar-restricted diets, so this might boost sales. An older child might be inspired to squeeze lemons to make fresh lemonade, which requires following a recipe and then pricing the ingredients she will need. Freshly squeezed lemonade could certainly be sold for more money.

How many glasses of lemonade does your daughter think she can sell at her stand? Fifty glasses? A hundred? Talking about this will help your daughter decide how much inventory to buy for her first day of sales.

These conversations demystify the business world. Your daughter will learn that effective ventures aren't magical guessing games; they are the result of careful planning and calculation. When your daughter learns that the more information she gathers beforehand about her business, the greater control she has over her sales and the more likely she is to make money, she will gain confidence and enjoy success.

Finally, tally up your expenditures. Encourage your daughter to watch the cashier scan the price of each packet of lemonade, set of cups, and pack of napkins. Show her the receipt and point out where each item is listed. Then explain that you're going to keep it and will talk about it later.

Practice Makes Perfect: Sales Presentation

Every good salesperson has to practice her sales pitch, so help your daughter hone hers. She's not going to sell much lemonade if she sits mutely at her table, eyes downcast, waiting for customers to come to her. Explain to her that selling is like catching fish. When you go out in a boat or sit on a pier, everyone knows the fish isn't going to just jump up and land—*kerplop!*—at your feet. You have to cast a line.

So pretend you're a customer walking toward her lemonade stand, and teach her how to reel in lemonade customers. Show her how to make eye contact, smile, and talk to you. Suggest that she talk loudly enough to be heard, engage in chatty conversation about the lemonade, and hold up a glass—people instinctively take a glass if it's offered to them. These seemingly small gestures will make a big difference in how much lemonade she sells and will dramatically increase her self-assurance and confidence. She will quickly see results from being outgoing and friendly, traits that will hold her in good stead in future businesses.

One question that always pops up is "What are you selling the lemonade for?" Adults will often be surprised that your daughter is in business for her own profit, as they are unaccustomed to a child asking for money for herself. Your daughter might be stumped by this, so help her prepare her answer, which is simply that she's in business to earn money for what she wants to buy—a bike, an iPod, whatever. Inevitably, the adult says, "Wow, I wish my kid would do that!"

An added benefit here is that teaching your children at a young age to communicate with adults gives them a great advantage. Children who are afraid of adults and don't interact with them often grow up to be fearful of authority in general.

Open for Business

The day has come for the grand opening of Sally's Yummy Pink Lemonade stand!

Go to the store and help your daughter set up her stand. Take a picture—this is a special day in her life, and you want to record it, as you do any other milestone, such as her first day at school or a birthday. Then remain in the background unless she needs your help. Depending on her age, she might need you to make change, replenish supplies, and handle some customer questions.

Your other reason for joining your daughter is to provide a cheering section on this important day. She will be facing the rigors of the marketplace—not everyone walking by is going to buy a glass of lemonade—and you can keep her enthusiasm up with lots of encouragement and positive reinforcement when she makes a sale. Don't hesitate to bring in ringers to boost sales. Your goal is for her to have a positive experience, no matter what. She will remember her good feelings about the day as much as she will savor the amount of money she made.

When it's time to shut up the shop for the day, suggest that she go inside and thank the manager; then help her clean up and bring home the profits!

Celebrate the Launch

When you get home, spread out all the money on the kitchen table so your daughter can see how much she's earned. Make a big fuss, and lay on the praise! Let the rest of the family gather around and exclaim over her success.

When she is glowing with pride at her achievements, bring out the receipts from the store where you bought the inventory and teach her the first lesson in gross and net profits by asking her to count out the money you spent for her ingredients. That money, you explain, will be used to buy more lemonade ingredients if she wants to run her lemonade stand another day. All the rest is her profit, which is hopefully a goodly sum if she followed all the business advice you gave her. That is her own money to spend as she pleases. If she wants, drive her to the store that very afternoon so she gets instant gratification from her work.

If your entrepreneur is a little bit older and her "want" is bigger, set up a visual representation of her want so that she can mark off her progress toward paying for it. A picture of a bike can be colored in as profits accrue until the whole bike is colored and all the money for its purchase is in your daughter's pocket.

Mission Accomplished

Congratulations to you both. Walking your child through a new business and seeing it launched is a major, major achievement for her, and also for you. You now have an enthusiastic young entrepreneur who has had her first taste of success. She came up with a business concept that interested her, and then she took the necessary steps to make it a reality. Most important for her, she earned some money on her own!

In future business meetings, you will continue to encourage and guide her as she faces some inevitable disappointments in the lemonade business, but she will become increasingly confident of her skills and of her ability to make them pay.

Your daughter may sell lemonade until she earns enough money to buy what she wants and then shut the business down until she has another "want," or she may continue pumping out that great-tasting lemonade because she is having fun and wants to continue to earn more money.

Whatever she does with her business is fine, because it's hers! Her ability to start and stop her business is one of the first truly empowering moments she will have as a young business owner. Let her enjoy this wonderful perk of control.

Keep in mind that this is just the beginning of your daughter's business career. She will almost certainly come up with more ideas about businesses she can start as she finds new passions and grows in maturity and confidence. Whatever she decides to do, please stay positive and supportive as long as the business fits within the moral and ethical boundaries of your household. All her choices are part of the journey toward being a future millionaire.

What you have taught her are many of the portable business skills that she will be able to use throughout her life. She has learned from this simple enterprise that imagination, planning, and hard work enable her to generate income for herself.

As her mentor, you will continue to encourage, listen, and support her business efforts as she gains confidence, expertise, and money. She will not always succeed—trying new businesses means taking risks that sometimes don't pay off—but with your help she will learn from her mistakes and persevere.

So go forth with your future millionaire, and enjoy the journey! You have given your young entrepreneur a great gift through your encouragement, practical advice, and support. And chances are, you've received pleasure in equal measure. Let your heart rejoice as you rest in the knowledge that you have given your own child the power and skills to take care of herself.

In the next chapters are some proven businesses for children of all ages. You will find some good ideas, not only for your child's first business, but for her second and third businesses. They should remain a reference guide for you and your child as she becomes accustomed to the need to create businesses to make the money she wants.

SEVEN

Big-Buck Businesses

GREAT ENTERPRISES: BASKET CASE TO GAME GURU

BY NOW, YOU AND YOUR FUTURE MILLIONAIRE HAVE SOME great business ideas—your son or daughter might even be making some nice profits from his or her first enterprise. As you are learning, there are many ways to make money when you match your child's abilities to some basic business skills and opportunities.

To further guide you and your young entrepreneur, I've put together a list of successful businesses for young people. There are all kinds of businesses here, so you're bound to find many that will suit your future millionaire. Some require very little start-up money; others require more, so you can select businesses with costs with which you're comfortable. I purposely haven't set any age requirements or limitations, because children's abilities vary so much. I have indicated some general traits that would be helpful for some of the businesses, but you know your own child better than anyone and can sort through these myriad choices with an eye to what would best suit your future millionaire. Most of all, each of them can be a lot of fun, and when your child takes advantage of the sound

71

business principles we've talked about in *Young Bucks*, he or she will be guaranteed some nice profits.

The list can serve as a jumping-off point for you and your child to brainstorm about other business opportunities. There are endless possibilities out there for your future millionaire if he puts on his thinking cap and does some homework.

Because I have outlined nearly thirty businesses, I've separated them into three chapters, arranged in alphabetical order, just to make the information a little easier to read.

BUSINESS TITLE: Basket Case

SUMMARY: Build and sell unique gift baskets

DETAILED DESCRIPTION: If you have ever received a gift basket, you have probably thought, "Wow, this was probably expensive!" and "There is some really cool stuff in here!"

There is always excitement in seeing a lot of small gifts packed into a big, fancy basket. No matter how old you are, it's like a little treasure hunt to discover what's tucked inside for you to unwrap. For a young entrepreneur, the happy discovery is that gift baskets can be assembled with very inexpensive items that, collectively, have great perceived value—which means he can charge more and have great profit margins! Your young entrepreneur can head to a local discount retailer or dollar store and pick up lots of items for themes that will suit his customers. He can decide what would be fun in a sports basket for an end-of-season present for a soccer champion, a graduation basket, a birthday basket, a Thanksgiving basket, and so on. People are used to paying considerable amounts for well-packaged gift baskets, and any child over the age of nine can assemble a great basket once he has been shown how.

START-UP COSTS: $100

MATERIALS NEEDED: The start-up money should be enough both to cover the cost of full-color business cards (with a photograph of a beautiful basket) and to buy the materials to assemble a sample basket.

POTENTIAL INCOME: $30 to $200 per basket!

SUGGESTED MARKETING STRATEGY: The majority of gift baskets are sent from one executive to another or from sales-people to valued customers, so your son's first stop should be at the desks of the secretaries and executive assistants of as many businesses as possible. These are the people who are usually in charge of making such purchases. Your future millionaire can build a strong relationship with them so they know that calling him will solve their need of a great gift for a great client.

But there are plenty of other occasions when a gift basket could be an appropriate gift: a teacher's gift at the end of the school year, something for the siblings of a new baby who's getting all the attention, a housewarming gift, and so on. The possibilities are endless for a child with an imagination and a flair for packaging.

BUSINESS TITLE: Better Air

SUMMARY: Clean/replace home/office air-conditioning filters

DETAILED DESCRIPTION: People often forget to rinse off or replace the filters in their air-conditioning systems at home and at work. Not doing so can lead to illness, much higher electric bills, and less comfortable homes. Offering to come by once a month to pull the filter, take it outside, and wash it out (or replace it with a new one every six months) is a true service with great value. Most people will gladly pay five to ten dollars to have someone perform this task for them. It only takes a few minutes and can be done on the spot. If your future millionaire hustles, she could do a dozen filters an hour, which is great money!

START-UP COSTS: $50 for a small assortment of filters to begin with

MATERIALS NEEDED: New air-conditioning filters, scrub brush, work gloves, disposable face mask (to avoid dust)

POTENTIAL INCOME: $20 to $125 per hour

SUGGESTED MARKETING STRATEGY: Your entrepreneur should memorize a few facts about the negative effects of having dirty air-conditioning filters—she can learn this information by talking with a local salesperson or looking on the Internet—and list the facts on a flyer. She can then take the flyers door-to-door and offer to clean the filter right on the spot. When she signs people up for a steady monthly service, she will soon find herself booked solid with recurring revenue every month!

BUSINESS TITLE: Braid & Paid

SUMMARY: Braid hair on location at special events and get paid per braid

DETAILED DESCRIPTION: Here is a great way for young girls to start a simple business with virtually no investment. (Of course, boys could start this business as well, but I am not one to be politically correct and don't think this business works as well when boys do it.) Many girls have learned the art of tight hair braiding and are good at weaving little accessories into these braids, adding a little flair to hair! I don't pretend to understand what makes this concept so appealing to girls of all ages, but it is very, very popular. If your daughter enjoys braiding her dolls' or her siblings' hair, then this may be the opportunity for her!

The potential for income is limited only by the speed at which your daughter can braid! If she can find two or three friends who also like to braid, she can double or triple her income! Finding a location for this business is easy. Anyplace crowds gather is a possible location, from the front of busy stores to a junior-high sporting event. If girls with hair are present, there is cash to be earned!

START-UP COSTS: Approximately $20 (the cost of accessories)

MATERIALS NEEDED: A couple of stools to sit on, some ribbon and miscellaneous braiding beads, etc.

POTENTIAL INCOME: $40 and up per hour! (Speed is key here.)

SUGGESTED MARKETING STRATEGY: One of the easiest ways to get started is to offer the service at a school sporting event. I suggest sharing the proceeds with the school booster club (not a 50/50 split—just a small percentage), and I recommend that your daughter braid hair with ribbons in the school colors. She could train other girls to work for her and then set them up at other schools in your community. On any given weekend, she could have four or five events (locations) going at once. The potential income from this business could be several hundred dollars in a single day! Girl Power!

BUSINESS TITLE: Can-Do

SUMMARY: Take out and return neighbors' trash cans

DETAILED DESCRIPTION: We all have to get our trash out to the curb before the garbage collectors get there early in the morning. Then when we get home, we need to gather up those empty, knocked-over cans and lids and get them back to the house. Some people frequently forget to get the trash out, or by the time they get home from work, the cans have rolled out into the street or neighborhood dogs have gotten into them. No more thinking about taking out the trash ever again. Your son can make a quick run through the neighborhood before school (like a paper route in the old days) and get all of the neighbors' trash cans hauled out to the curb. Then after school he can return the now-empty cans to their proper places.

START-UP COSTS: $10 for flyers

MATERIALS NEEDED: Homemade flyers to advertise your service

POTENTIAL INCOME: $20 and up per day

SUGGESTED MARKETING STRATEGY: This is a case study in good old-fashioned salesmanship. Your son should go door-to-door (with a parent in tow) and offer the service on a one-time, free-trial basis. Once people have enjoyed *not* taking their trash to the curb and then returning home after work and *not* seeing their trash cans scattered across the street, they will be hooked. A small fee of three to four dollars per trash day per customer adds up quickly. (If your son charges four dollars, he will be surprised at how many people just give him a five-dollar bill and tell him to keep the change!) Get ten nearby customers, and your son will make thirty to forty bucks for about an hour of work every trash day!

BUSINESS TITLE: Camper Pamper

SUMMARY: Clean up RVs and other hard-to-maintain vehicles

DETAILED DESCRIPTION: This is an auto-detailing business, but aimed at a more specific, usually overlooked niche. There are millions of RVs, big rigs, buses, and other large vehicles that need to be cleaned. If your child is really good at cleaning his room and doing other sorts of household chores, this may be the bucket of gold he is looking for. People with large vehicles usually hate to clean them up and will pay someone generously who can clean really well! You don't need a driver's license to clean a vehicle. My own son has had a business like this since he was fourteen and makes extremely good money doing it. The best thing about Camper Pamper is the high number of repeat customers—these big vehicles are in use constantly and therefore get dirty over and over! A repeat business like this means less time spent out marketing for new clients.

START-UP COSTS: Approximately $50 to $75 for cleaning supplies

MATERIALS NEEDED: Household cleaning chemicals, towels, vacuum (or access to a car wash with good vacuums)

POTENTIAL INCOME: $125 to $200 per vehicle. (You should be able to do one per day by yourself and two or three vehicles per day with a little help.)

SUGGESTED MARKETING STRATEGY: Nothing fancy is required here. Young entrepreneurs should draw up a flyer and slip copies under the window wipers of qualifying vehicles. Handing them out at truck stops in the community and near campgrounds is also a good idea. The local RV dealers and service centers will also be a great source of leads and may even become customers.

BUSINESS TITLE: Card Kid

SUMMARY: Send out greeting cards for others

DETAILED DESCRIPTION: This is a perfect kid-friendly business because it can be done anytime, even in front of the TV! It is also one that has been around for decades, but nobody talks about it because nobody wants to admit they use such a service. But I will confess—I have used a card-sending service for several years. All I do is provide a list of names and addresses of people I want to send cards to, along with the dates of important events in each person's life. My secret card sender tracks those dates, and when they get close, she sends out the card (she had me prewrite personal notes months earlier) and I never think about it again. I get a bill for the cards, postage, and a small convenience fee of thirty cents per card sent. It's very nice to get calls from people thanking me for the kind card that arrived just in time for the special event.

Businesses have hundreds, sometimes thousands, of customers to whom they send cards for birthdays, anniversaries, special sales, and so on. The woman who does my cards sends out hundreds of cards a day for numerous clients!

START-UP COSTS: $100

MATERIALS NEEDED: A variety of cards, some postage, and business cards for yourself

POTENTIAL INCOME: $0.25 to $0.50 per card mailed

SUGGESTED MARKETING STRATEGY: It's sometimes hard to get referrals from this business, because satisfied customers don't want to admit they use the service. So your best bet is to contact busy people, such as doctors, dentists, and car sales-people, and offer the service to them. Be sure to help them understand that the people important to them will *always* get a birthday, anniversary, graduation, or thank-you card on time, every time, automatically. This service is especially valuable to salespeople who really want to give their clients a personal touch but don't have the time to do it themselves!

BUSINESS TITLE: Compu-Kid

SUMMARY: Help adults with their computers

DETAILED DESCRIPTION: It is said that if Bill Gates would staff his entire tech support department with kids ages ten to fifteen, all computer problems could be fixed immediately! There is definitely some truth in this statement. Children today have been born and raised in a technological world. They have never known life without high-tech electronics and video game systems. Why not empower your whiz kid by allowing her to use her talents to help adults in the community with their PC problems? This business can cover everything from helping people set up the new computer they just bought to teaching them how to navigate the Internet, use instant messaging, and even hook up and download pictures from a digital camera. There are millions of adults who have no clue how to do all of these things, and they would be happy to pay your daughter to help them!

START-UP COSTS: $30 for business cards and flyers

MATERIALS NEEDED: Business cards and flyers

POTENTIAL INCOME: $20 to $50 per hour!

SUGGESTED MARKETING STRATEGY: Your daughter should begin by talking about her business in every social circle she has (and you have)—work, church, barber, and so on. Also post flyers in senior-dominant neighborhoods. *Bonus tip*: Stand outside one of the big-box electronics stores, such as Best Buy or Circuit City, and hand flyers to people carrying out computers or walking in with one to return!

BUSINESS TITLE: Cookie Club

SUMMARY: Organize a weekly cookie club to learn how to bake many different kinds of cookies.

DETAILED DESCRIPTION: Who doesn't love cookies? Well, imagine a club in which you could learn to make all different kinds of cookies and then eat them! If your child is interested in cookies and cooking, this could be a terrific business. Your future millionaire can recruit a group of children to join her for a weekly class to make cookies and take home the results as well as a new recipe. She could also use this cookie club as a staff for baking enough cookies to sell around town, and the club members would share the resulting revenue. So it is a club but also a business with employees. (And everyone gets to eat cookies!)

If the baker is particularly accomplished, she could market the class to adults as well—lots of moms like to learn to make new desserts.

START-UP COSTS: $10 to $15 per class for ingredients, heavy-stock index cards, cookie boxes

MATERIALS NEEDED: A kitchen, which could be at your home, church, school, or a local community center; cookie ingredients; recipe cards for everyone to write down the recipe; containers for the club members to take their cookies home. (You might get the containers from a Chinese restaurant—cute and just the right size for a sample of the cookies.)

POTENTIAL INCOME: $15 to 40 per student per month. (This does *not* include revenue from cookies sold directly to the public!)

SUGGESTED MARKETING STRATEGY: Distribute flyers to families in the neighborhood and anyplace parents of younger children can be targeted. Some schools may even let you send a flyer home with students. Also rely on church newsletters, community message boards, and simple word of mouth. Selling cookies in front of stores will also increase enrollment in the cookie club if a sign-up sheet is available on the sales table.

BUSINESS TITLE: Game Guru

SUMMARY: Facilitate fun games at children's parties

DETAILED DESCRIPTION: Planning a kid's birthday is a big deal to parents. A lot of thought goes into the cake, gifts, decorations, and invitations—and *then* the parents have to figure out what the kids are going to do!

Party-planning parents want to make sure everyone has a great time at their child's birthday party . . . and this is where your son comes in. He knows better than most parents what kids like to do, and if he becomes an expert on dozens of games for all ages—from quiet, indoor games to outdoor games using the water hose, balloons, relay races, and so on—he will have a business bonanza.

This business is great for an outgoing, self-assured child who isn't afraid to be silly and have fun while working with the children. He should also learn a few simple line dances and camp-type songs that can be taught quickly and easily.

START-UP COSTS: $50

MATERIALS NEEDED: Business cards (flyers would also be helpful) and, initially, several books, either purchased or checked out from the library, containing lots of games and activities for different age groups

POTENTIAL INCOME: $50 to $200 per party!

SUGGESTED MARKETING STRATEGY: As soon as possible, your son should offer his services to someone free of charge to jump-start his marketing. At this event, you should take lots of pictures of him interacting with the other children, shots of them laughing and participating. Then have the parent of the birthday child write a glowing endorsement for your future millionaire. Finally, put the best pictures and the testimonial into a flyer, and your son can start distributing them to parents at the local soccer field on Saturday morning. He will be amazed how many calls are on the answering machine when he gets home!

EIGHT

More Big-Buck Businesses

GREAT ENTERPRISES: GOPHER GIRL
TO RENT-A-SCRAP

BUSINESS TITLE: Gopher Girl (or Guy)

SUMMARY: Run errands

DETAILED DESCRIPTION: Everyone has many mundane and repeating errands—we all know what they are. There is no convenient time to do them, but you're still stuck doing them regardless . . . *unless* there is a Gopher Girl in your area! Your son or daughter of driving age can run errands for busy people who don't want to leave the office during the day. For some it will be as simple as dropping off dry cleaning and picking up prescriptions. But for others it can be an entire grocery list, birthday shopping, and an oil change! If your future millionaire finds a good office building or heavily staffed office, he will stay swamped just keeping those people's errands taken care of!

START-UP COSTS: $25 for business cards

MATERIALS NEEDED: A car, a cell phone, and fuel

POTENTIAL INCOME: $25 to $50 per hour!

SUGGESTED MARKETING STRATEGY: It's all about the business card on this one. Get a high-quality card printed on heavy card stock (or a magnet) so it will last a long time. Your daughter should put her name and cell phone number on the front, along with the title Gopher Girl. Then on the back, she should list as many typical errands as she can think of—the more the better.

When she hands the card to someone, she can tell that person how she will free up his valuable time by running his errands for him. She should make sure to flip the card over when she gives it to a potential customer and show that customer the list. She can then ask the potential client to call her if he needs help. At the same time, your daughter should make her own list of everyone to whom she gives a card and make regular follow-up calls to see if she can help them do anything that day. She will be surprised how many people will say yes!

BUSINESS TITLE: Great Grout

SUMMARY: Scrub and clean the grout on tile floors and showers

DETAILED DESCRIPTION: Here is another example of how to make big money doing things other people don't want to do. Grout is that stuff between the tiles on a floor or bathroom shower wall. Those "lines" don't come clean just from a quick mop down. Cleaning them requires getting down on your knees and scrubbing them with a sturdy brush. The reason this is such a lucrative business has to do with a *single word* in that previous sentence: *knees!* Very few adults want to get down on their tired, sore knees and scrub anything—they would rather pay your child to do it. Kids can do this sort of work quite well and surprisingly fast! Not a lot of thinking involved in this one—just good old elbow grease! This is a perfect kid-friendly business for a conscientious child who's a hard worker.

START-UP COSTS: $25 or less

MATERIALS NEEDED: A couple of sturdy scrub brushes and cleaning chemicals

POTENTIAL INCOME: $1 per square foot ($50 per hour and up!)

SUGGESTED MARKETING STRATEGY: Put together an album of before-and-after photos, taken close up, including pictures of your future millionaire doing the work! If your child takes this simple photo album around to neighbors and lets them see the results for themselves, he will get hired. When he's finished with a job, he should ask every customer for a written testimonial and the names of three friends who have tile.

BUSINESS TITLE: Leftover Fortunes

SUMMARY: Collect remaining merchandise from garage sales and sell it on eBay

DETAILED DESCRIPTION: For the girl who loves to spend time on the Internet, this little business can be one of the more profitable there is! On any given Saturday, your daughter can grab a digital camera and the newspaper and wait for lunch to be over. Then she can hit the trail of garage sales in the community. By lunchtime, the rush of bargain hunters has come and gone, and the people trying to sell their old stuff are getting tired of sitting outside. They will take almost any offer for whatever they have left. Your child can buy it for next to nothing. She then snaps a picture of it, sets up an online auction (eBay or one of the many others), and lets the bidding begin! There are several ways to make a profit, from selling the merchandise for more than she paid for it to keeping the purchase price low but raising the price for shipping and handling. She can put hundreds of auctions up and make much of her profit from the shipping and handling charges!

START-UP COSTS: $200

MATERIALS NEEDED: A decent digital camera and enough money to buy some "stuff"

POTENTIAL INCOME: $50 to $500 per day!

SUGGESTED MARKETING STRATEGY: The details described previously are basically all the marketing strategy your young entrepreneur needs. However, an additional suggestion would be for her to approach people before they have a garage sale and tell them they could avoid the hassle and hard work of having a sale by letting her place all of their best stuff on an Internet auction. Instead of setting up and advertising their sale, they have your future millionaire come to their house, take pictures of what they want to sell, and launch the auction. Then she shares the revenues with the sellers.

BUSINESS TITLE: Meal Builder

SUMMARY: Prepare meals from a customer's own recipes

DETAILED DESCRIPTION: Most people will agree that nothing beats a good old-fashioned home-cooked meal. But today's fast-paced life leaves very little time to prepare such a feast. Your son, who loves to cook, can take advantage of this time shortage. Busy people simply hand him the recipes they want to enjoy (torn from magazines or from their own family recipes) and tell him which nights they want them and at what time. He (with your assistance) picks up the groceries, prepares the meal per the recipe, and either delivers it at the specified time or arranges for the customer to pick it up on the way home from work. Your son is paid for the cost of the groceries as well as a preparation fee! It's like having a restaurant without the hassle of owning it!

START-UP COSTS: $25

MATERIALS NEEDED: Business cards and flyers

POTENTIAL INCOME: $20 to $50 per meal

SUGGESTED MARKETING STRATEGY: This business has potential for tremendous growth. Your son can distribute flyers and/or call on potential customers—well-paid, busy people—and offer to prepare one of the customer's own recipes for free, minus the cost of the ingredients. He can tell them he wants them to experience the service and taste his cooking. More times than not, a busy and hungry customer will be curious and take him up on the offer. Once a too-busy person has enjoyed one of his own favorite recipes with no effort on his part, he will be your son's newest customer! It only takes a handful of customers to keep your son very busy. Once there is a client for every night of the week, he can start raising the prices to meet the demand!

BUSINESS TITLE: Movie Mogul

SUMMARY: Convert old VHS tapes to DVDs

DETAILED DESCRIPTION: All of us adults have boxes of old VHS tapes that are slowly deteriorating in the attic, basement, or extra closet. Getting them converted to digital is important if we want to keep them for our children and grandchildren to enjoy. But who has the time and know-how to do that? Well, with two minutes of training, your child does! New, inexpensive, and easy-to-use DVD converting machines are for sale in any electronics store or superstore. Your young entrepreneur can buy one of these machines, plug it in, and start copying and converting. The potential customer base is huge! The work is easy and is ideal for a child who may not be interested in a more people-oriented, sales business. This task can be done privately at home, and except for dropping off the new DVDs and getting the check, there is no need to chat. Fun, easy, and profitable.

START-UP COSTS: About $150 to $200 for a good recording unit

MATERIALS NEEDED: Business cards and a VHS/DVD converter

POTENTIAL INCOME: $5 to $25 per DVD burned

SUGGESTED MARKETING STRATEGY: The people who are most worried about the slow deterioration of their old tapes are those with children or grandchildren. So the best source of leads is going to be other parents like you. Have your child pass out her business cards to parents after school at the parent pick-up area, and watch the phone start ringing. If your daughter offers to do some free copying for the school principal, that satisfied customer may allow her to send home a flyer with the children—especially if she offers to give part of her profits to the school.

BUSINESS TITLE: On My Honor

SUMMARY: Place boxes of candy for sale in trustworthy environments where people help themselves and pay on the honor system

DETAILED DESCRIPTION: This is one of those businesses I never would have guessed would actually work until I witnessed it firsthand with my own children. A young entrepreneur places various types of popular candy bars into an open box or display container (homemade is best) with an attached sign stating the price and the honor system. Next to the candy box is another, sealed money box for payment. The boxes are then placed (with proper permission) at places where honesty should not be an issue. These could be places like parents' offices, the local barbershop or hair salon, a car dealership, or the break room at a law office. Believe it or not, not only do people usually pay for their candy, but some overpay! My own son did this at age six. He had four locations and netted about $100 a week—not bad for a six-year-old!

START-UP COSTS: Approximately $20 for the candy

MATERIALS NEEDED: Candy, cardboard display box, sealed money box

POTENTIAL INCOME: $25 and up per box per week

SUGGESTED MARKETING STRATEGY: Great locations are key here. Decorating the box with a photo of the child is also important. This shows people that the business is owned by a child, and what kind of person is going to cheat a child?

BUSINESS TITLE: Party Pics

SUMMARY: Take pictures at events and offer them for sale

DETAILED DESCRIPTION: No matter how advanced our technological society has gotten, people still love to have photos to remember special events. An interested preteen or teen armed with a decent digital camera can make a very nice business out of party pictures. Simply offer to come to a person's party, either a child or an adult function, and snap pictures of the guests and events all day or night long. School events, sporting events, grand openings, and business conferences are all potential venues. Your future millionaire can charge a flat fee for coming and taking the pictures and then just turn over the digital files when she's finished, or she can either sell prints to attendees before they leave or arrange to deliver them at a later date.

START-UP COSTS: $100 to $400

MATERIALS NEEDED: Digital camera, access to a computer with quality printer, photo paper, flyers

POTENTIAL INCOME: $50 to $500 per event. Good pictures of special moments have significant value to some people.

SUGGESTED MARKETING STRATEGY: A decorative photo album filled with good party/event pictures taken by your daughter and a few testimonial letters from satisfied customers (an uncle or a friendly neighbor will be fine) will launch your young photographer. She can distribute flyers and follow up with visits to show her album and offer to photograph their next event. Knowing when the neighborhood children are having birthday parties helps, as does keeping up with church or school calendars for events that she could photograph.

BUSINESS TITLE: Play for Pay

SUMMARY: Demonstrate new games for pay

DETAILED DESCRIPTION: Companies are constantly developing new games and toys for children and need people to demonstrate in public just how fun those new games can be. Some game distributors will pay kids (generally ages twelve and up) to spend time at various retailers, demonstrating the game. Compensation varies from an hourly wage to a commission based on sales. I suggest the latter. This is a great business for an outgoing child who loves games and having fun.

START-UP COSTS: Under $25

MATERIALS NEEDED: Business card and eventually a résumé of companies that hired the future millionaire to play games

POTENTIAL INCOME: $20 to $100 per day

SUGGESTED MARKETING STRATEGY: Your son, with your help, can contact the local game distributors in your city and let them know that he would like to demonstrate new products. The company rep will generally want to meet him to see what sort of personality and sales ability he has. Once he is convinced to give him a try, he will train him on a product and assign him to a retail location to do his thing! Your child may have to do more work here than in some other businesses to persuade the company to give him a chance, but once his ability is proven, the sky is the limit! Your son can be selling products at the flea market, home parties, and on-site at every major retailer in town that carries the product.

BUSINESS TITLE: Rent-a-Friend

SUMMARY: Provide companionship to older people

DETAILED DESCRIPTION: The idea of paying for friendship might seem odd to some, but it is actually a very popular service that is both gratifying and economically rewarding. Because of distance, time constraints, or other logistics, people whose elderly parents are either in nursing homes or living alone cannot always visit them as often as they would like, and a regularly scheduled visit from a kind teen is a godsend. A sympathetic young person who will sit and read a good book, play a game of chess, or just talk about the day's events can be the highlight of a lonely person's day. This is a kinder, gentler way of offering an elderly sitter service, but without the responsibility of any medical or personal care. A good business for a sensitive and compassionate young person.

START-UP COSTS: $25

MATERIALS NEEDED: Business cards

POTENTIAL INCOME: $10 to $25 per hour

SUGGESTED MARKETING STRATEGY: Due to the nature of this business, it is best to utilize the human network rather than relying on a fancy marketing program. Your daughter can visit a local nursing home, speak to the activities director, and ask to put a notice in the facility's newsletter, which is sent out to the residents' families. She could also let her church know that she would like to offer her services—people often use local churches for social service resources. If coordinated, your daughter may have several clients at the same nursing home whom she could visit in an afternoon.

While this is a somewhat atypical business for a young entrepreneur, it is very much needed, and families are extremely grateful to a caring young person who brings some light into their relative's life. Further, unlike some of the other businesses outlined here, the relationship your child will have with an elderly person will have a profound emotional impact on her for many years to come.

BUSINESS TITLE: Rent-a-Scrap

SUMMARY: Create and assemble scrapbooks for busy people.

DETAILED DESCRIPTION: No matter how busy some working parents are, every mom or dad I have ever known takes numerous photos of the children over the years—vacations, birthdays, graduations, and so on. But very, very few parents ever find the time to dump all of those pictures and keepsakes onto the floor and catalog them into an organized and attractive scrapbook. That reality can be converted into an exciting and extremely lucrative business for any crafty young boy or girl.

START-UP COSTS: $50 and up

MATERIALS NEEDED: Various scrapbooking supplies and business cards

POTENTIAL INCOME: $100 to $500 per completed scrapbook

SUGGESTED MARKETING STRATEGY: This one is easy to market—have your daughter build a scrapbook with examples of her very best work and carry it everywhere she goes to show to potential customers. You can help, too, by showing her work to your friends who have boxes stuffed with unsorted photographs and explaining how much your daughter loves to convert other people's boxes of old photos into beautiful, keepsake-quality scrapbooks.

People may be embarrassed to have someone else try to make sense of the mess in their old shoe boxes, but your daughter (and you) can reassure the potential customer that having others build a scrapbook is a growing trend, and disorganized boxes of photos are part of the process. Once a couple of satisfied clients are out in the community, your daughter will be flooded with business and may need to hire help!

NINE

Even More Big-Buck Businesses

GREAT ENTERPRISES: SHOOT-FOR-LOOT TO WONDER WINDOWS

BUSINESS TITLE: Shoot-for-Loot

SUMMARY: Photography for hire

DETAILED DESCRIPTION: With today's amazing digital technology, cameras have become so smart that it is difficult to take a bad picture. And what cameras can't do, software can! Many of today's kids are already experts at manipulating pictures to amuse their friends; why not encourage them to do the same thing for grown-ups?

Imagine being told by a young photographer that she can take your family's picture and *then* go in and whiten everybody's teeth, trim off a double chin, and remove the shine from Grandpa's bald head! In the past, those services were very costly and quite time-consuming. Today's software allows almost anyone who will take the time to learn to edit and touch up photos like a pro! Let your creative and technologically adept daughter take that time to teach herself to use the software and start her own business.

START-UP COSTS: $200

MATERIALS NEEDED: Decent camera and editing software

POTENTIAL INCOME: $50 to $500 per customer

SUGGESTED MARKETING STRATEGY: A single photograph! That's what a young photographer will need to drum up all of the business she could ever want. Have her take a photo of a group of people and then touch up as many things as possible—faces, bodies, and background. Then have her put the before-and-after photos on a flyer with her name and contact information. Post those flyers anywhere you're allowed to post them. People will start calling almost immediately asking for pricing, availability, and so on. If your daughter enjoys taking pictures and manipulating photos (as she does for her friends), this business may stay with her for a lifetime!

BUSINESS TITLE: Sitter University

SUMMARY: Teach other kids how to be successful babysitters

DETAILED DESCRIPTION: Parents are always looking for responsible, competent babysitters. At the same time, there are young people out there who want to *be* good babysitters but don't really know the tricks of the trade to become an in-demand sitter. A young entrepreneur with babysitting experience can hold monthly classes for potential sitters who come in for a half day and learn all there is to know about babysitting: how to amuse children, what housekeeping chores are part of babysitting, what *not* to do while babysitting (like inviting friends over), how much to charge, and so on. Also a possibility is inviting a Red Cross representative to the training session to teach infant CPR.

When the training is completed, your daughter can provide students with a certificate that they can tell potential clients they have earned. Additionally, your daughter can get the word out that through her "Sitter University," she can provide babysitters for parents. As the business grows and she has a roster of trained babysitters, she could charge an annual fee to parents who could call her anytime and get a babysitter.

START-UP COSTS: $25 for business cards and blank certificates

MATERIALS NEEDED: blank certificates (available at Office Depot) and simple business cards or flyers

POTENTIAL INCOME: $25 per student

SUGGESTED MARKETING STRATEGY: Through flyers and word of mouth, your future millionaire can spread the word about her business to parents at school, local churches, and day care centers. She can also hand out flyers and tell other teens that there is money to be made if they go through her training successfully. She should be sure to take a few flyers with her to the mall to hand to teens, and when she tags along with you to the grocery store, she can pass out flyers to all of the mothers in the baby food aisle!

BUSINESS TITLE: Son Shine

SUMMARY: Provide a shoe-shine service

DETAILED DESCRIPTION: Everybody has shoes, but not everyone's shoes look good. In fact, if you look down as you walk along the street, you will see an awful lot of scruffy, unpolished, and sloppy-looking footwear. That's because people never get around to polishing their shoes, either because they don't have the time or equipment or because there are very few places to get shoes shined—I usually only see shoe-shine stations at the airport. But if someone makes it convenient to keep shoes clean and buffed, most people, especially businesspeople, for whom neat appearances are important, will take advantage of the service. Enter your young entrepreneur and his very lucrative shoe-shine business! Portable shoe-shine kits are available at numerous Web sites, and you can even assemble your own. Easy to learn, easy to do, easy to find customers!

START-UP COSTS: $50

MATERIALS NEEDED: Shoe-shine supplies

POTENTIAL INCOME: $50 per hour!

SUGGESTED MARKETING STRATEGY: This is a great repeat business and a lot of fun for a sociable and competent young worker because he sees his clients regularly, and they are happy to see him and even tip him a little extra for a job well done. Once he has mastered the art of polishing shoes to a bright shine, he can make up flyers that explain his service, which includes coming to an office or shop once a week to either shine on-site or pick up shoes and return them polished and clean. If customers opt for on-site work, your son can set up in the break room of any busy office and have people bring in their shoes and leave them to be shined. While the staff are walking around in their socks, your son is in the back room, shining away! When finished, he tosses them all into his wagon and rolls around the offices, returning the shined shoes and picking up his money.

If he is able to drum up more shoes than he can shine in a short period of time, he bags up the shoes, takes them all home to shine (or hires others to help), and then returns them in a couple of days, all shined and ready to be worn. This business can get very big very fast if enough offices sign up for the service. I suggest going to law firms and real estate offices first.

BUSINESS TITLE: Sprinkle Bell

SUMMARY: Water and feed plants for people

DETAILED DESCRIPTION: As you look around inside lovely homes and offices, you will find many beautiful plants . . . that desperately need water! Too often plants are the victims of environments filled with busy people who don't have time to take proper care of their plants. If your daughter likes plants, this is the job for her! By dropping by on a regular schedule and properly watering and feeding the plants throughout an office or home, your daughter is providing a much-needed service that has a documented track record of being lucrative. And everyone will be so happy to see their flora looking healthy and thriving, and so relieved that they don't have to take care of their plants themselves, that they will greet your daughter with big smiles.

START-UP COSTS: $50

MATERIALS NEEDED: Watering can, plant-care supplies, and business cards

POTENTIAL INCOME: $10 to $50 per office per visit!

SUGGESTED MARKETING STRATEGY: Your future millionaire should always keep her eye out—for *death*! Dead or dying plants are a sure sign of a potential client! Whenever she (or you) visits an office or is out shopping, she should leave her business card with any person whose office or home has plants. Also, when out watering plants at any office complex, she should drop by every nearby neighbor to let them know she is available to care for their plants and could do it right now or the next time she comes by. Spontaneous service is a great way to earn an instant client.

BUSINESS TITLE: Team Spirit Patrol

SUMMARY: Sell customized merchandise as a middleman

DETAILED DESCRIPTION: If your son or daughter is a good salesperson, this is a great business opportunity! People love to wear, write with, and surround themselves with the brands they work and live around. For example, students and school-teachers often wear T-shirts and sweatshirts with the school's logo. Employees have office items with their employer's logo on it. When presented with the personalized merchandise right in front of them, most people will purchase something, especially when it is priced low and is being sold by a sincere child.

You can help your future millionaire with this business. While no special expertise is needed, you can guide him to identify some likely venues where personalized T-shirts, mouse pads, socks, ties, and so on, would be popular—schools, small businesses, and so on—then help him find a company that sells these kinds of products (most easily on the Internet). Once he finds a few good vendors, he should select some unique products that he could sell. These companies' catalogs usually offer items in bulk for a low cost. Your future millionaire will be the middleman, supplying a business with personalized products that they, in turn, can either sell or give to customers.

START-UP COSTS: $100

MATERIALS NEEDED: With this business, your start-up costs will include a unique sample of what you're selling, such as a personalized paperweight or a pen holder that will capture the fancy of a potential client. You can then sell it as part of your first order.

POTENTIAL INCOME: The sky is the limit on this one!

SUGGESTED MARKETING STRATEGY: The best bet with this business is for your young entrepreneur to show his product up front to potential customers. Preprint something in a small quantity with a particular company's logo on it and walk in the office, offering the product for sale. A safe bet is usually a dozen mouse pads. They can be printed for a couple of dollars apiece, and your future millionaire can sell them for four or five times what he paid for them. It is a quick and tidy profit, as well as a foot in the door to offer even more customized products.

At school, your child can test the waters with a simple customized product that does not compete with anything already sold in the school store or through the booster club—perhaps something special, just for teachers and administrators. If it's low-cost and unique, they will buy it and use it proudly. Your son may even become the custom printer of choice for future school shirts, hats, and so on. Remember, this business does not require any skills other than salesmanship!

BUSINESS TITLE: Tutor Tots

SUMMARY: Teach younger children topics of your expertise.

DETAILED DESCRIPTION: We all have something we are better at than others, and the same goes for our children. So determine what your child is good at, and let her teach someone else—child or adult. Your daughter could teach younger children the same school subjects that a traditional tutor would teach—reading, writing, and math. But she could also teach adults or even seniors things like how to use the Internet, burn music CDs, set up an iPod, use the advanced features on a cell phone—the list goes on and on. Self-confident children who are comfortable around younger kids or adults are good candidates for this business.

START-UP COSTS: $25

MATERIALS NEEDED: Business cards

POTENTIAL INCOME: $25 per tutoring session (Some gigs will be a one-time tutoring session, while others will be ongoing/recurring sessions.)

SUGGESTED MARKETING STRATEGY: On her business card, in bullet format, your future millionaire should list all of the topics she is qualified to tutor. Then encourage her to speak openly to all of the adults she knows about her business. These adults will either use her services themselves or know somebody who could benefit from them. When she hears of such folks, she should ask for their telephone numbers and go straight home to call them and offer to help. People don't routinely ask for outside help but welcome it when it's needed.

BUSINESS TITLE: The Undertaker of the Forest

SUMMARY: Remove and dispose of Christmas trees

DETAILED DESCRIPTION: Each year, millions of Christmas trees are sold, decorated, then undecorated and . . . "What do we do with this dead tree?" Getting it out of the house is a big chore, and then the dried and shedding tree needs to be hauled to the curb or to a dump. As the official undertaker of Christmas trees, your teenage son (or daughter) will be able to provide a *much-needed* service during the holiday season—and earn some *much-needed* cash. The ideal way to provide this service is to come in and trim the tree down to a manageable size, bag it, haul it out, and then vacuum the remaining pine needles. Your customer will have been spared the mess, the sticky sap, and the scratches from carrying it and will have the peace of mind of knowing ahead of time that it will all be taken care of. No more dreading the take-down of the Christmas tree. (This annual business can also lead to opportunities to do other odd jobs for customers who have now seen your hardworking future millionaire in action.)

START-UP COSTS: $10 for protective gloves and big bags to carry out the trees

MATERIALS NEEDED: Business cards (shaped like a tree or a tombstone)

POTENTIAL INCOME: $10 per tree

SUGGESTED MARKETING STRATEGY: Pass out cards at the closest tree vendor and at busy shopping centers. Several days before Christmas, hang door tags that say, "The Tree Undertaker will be passing through your neighborhood Wednesday, December 30, to remove your Christmas tree. If you want yours taken out, please hang this tag back on your door on December 29." Then you cruise through the neighborhood, stopping at every house with a tag on the door and picking up a tree and a ten-dollar bill!

BUSINESS TITLE: We Do Weeds

SUMMARY: Pull weeds for pay

DETAILED DESCRIPTION: This one is a no-brainer. People generally hate pulling weeds from their gardens and landscaping. Find something people hate to do and you have found a potential revenue opportunity. Pulling weeds is simple work that children of almost any age (certainly seven and up) can do with very little training. It's a dirty job, but that's why people will pay to have it done.

START-UP COSTS: $5

MATERIALS NEEDED: Trash bags and work gloves

POTENTIAL INCOME: $10 to $100 per day. Charge by the job, not by the hour, using your common sense to set a fair price. A seven-year-old who's clearing the small beds on each side of the front door could charge about $10, for instance, enough for an hour's work and a fortune to a young child. Imagine a space the size of your child's own sleeping bed. That space, sprinkled with weeds, should earn around $10. However, that same space filled with many weeds should be worth at least $15, as it will take much longer to do and is a much dirtier job.

SUGGESTED MARKETING STRATEGY: Your child should go door-to-door (always with a parent close by) only to the homes where there are visible weeds that need attention. She can knock on the door with work gloves already on her hands and holding a big open trash bag. When she looks ready to go to work, people will make a spontaneous decision to just say, "Sure. Pull them out!"

BUSINESS TITLE: Wonder Windows

SUMMARY: Wash windows

DETAILED DESCRIPTION: The good news is that every home and car in the world has windows. The better news is that most people loathe washing them. The best news is that any child with a little patience can be taught how to clean a window! It requires very little training, only a handful of supplies, low start-up costs, and there is repeat business week after week, month after month!

START-UP COSTS: $25

MATERIALS NEEDED: business cards (I suggest clear plastic to resemble a window), glass cleaner, and old newspapers (my preferred glass-wiping product)

POTENTIAL INCOME: $5 to $50 per customer

SUGGESTED MARKETING STRATEGY: Children can walk into a business or home (with adults, for safety), offer their business cards, and ask for permission to clean a window for free to demonstrate their window-cleaning skills. When your child is given permission to clean a free window, he should select a dirty or spotted window and then clean *half* of it! This allows the potential client to see for himself what a difference your child can make. Most people don't realize how dirty their windows are until they see them cleaned. If your son targets the car window market, he should clean the portion of the windshield that is directly in front of the driver's seat—that way, even if they don't do business with him initially, potential customers will be forced to look through the clean window every day and be reminded of what a good job he did. As long as they have his card, he will hear back from them eventually!

TEN

Business Pitfalls

SUCKER-PROOF YOUR FUTURE MILLIONAIRE

RAISING A FUTURE MILLIONAIRE MEANS NOT ONLY nurturing his creativity and teaching him basic skills, but alerting him to the dishonesty and even fraud that can lurk amid the bounty of the business world. We teach our children skills to protect them from harm in their daily lives—*don't take rides from strangers, don't walk home alone from school after dark*, and so on—and a business mentor must do the same for his young entrepreneur. While teaching our kids to be optimistic is crucial to their success when starting a new venture, we are not being responsible parents if we don't also show them how to recognize and protect themselves from adults who have no compunction about trying to cheat children.

Equally important is helping them develop a healthy skepticism about get-rich-quick schemes whose aim is not to help them earn money, but to take it away!

If your future millionaire is under six, you must shield him from these problems, because he is too young and trusting to understand that the world isn't a good place. Even if he did know, he couldn't do anything about it—he needs your protection.

Sadly, any school-age child has already learned that not everyone is honest. He's seen the boy who takes more than his share of cookies at snack time, the girl who never plays by the rules at recess, and the classmate who blamed him for something she had done, though *he* got the punishment. He now understands that while most kids play fair, there are always a few whom you can't trust.

He, too, needs some protection but is sophisticated enough to apply what he's learned in school to his business career so he can protect himself from being disappointed and losing money.

People Problems

Most adults will buy just about anything a child is selling in an effort to support that youngster's drive and ambition. This is one of the most compelling reasons for teaching your child about business at an early age, in fact, because he will generally find the world a welcoming place.

Not all adults are supportive, however. It frustrates me, for instance, to see insensitive adults pass by a young businessman without so much as an encouraging glance or a positive word. But this is part of the learning curve. Your child has to understand that not everyone is going to be his cheerleader, and his disappointment will turn into resilience as he faces occasional indifference.

But it is a very serious (and infuriating!) matter to encounter adults who will intentionally cheat a child out of money. This does happen, and you must look after your child, especially if she is young. Always help her double-check her numbers when counting money, make sure her paperwork is in order, and assist in keeping track of her inventory. Allow her to be the "boss," but act as a good shadow employee and her watchdog.

When you discover something shady, don't force your child to confront the offending adult. You handle the dirty work, but later explain what happened so your child understands what was dishonest, how you handled it, and what the outcome was. This will prepare her for the time when she has to deal with it herself.

Following are some of the most common types of dishonest adults whom your future millionaire, like any businessperson, is likely to encounter when launching a career.

The Power Tripper

Negotiation is a learned skill that improves over time, which is why adults are generally much better negotiators than children (although my six-year-old, Trendon, is brilliant at negotiating his way out of naps!). Most adults dealing with children realize this and will restrain themselves when making deals with young entrepreneurs. There will always be a few, however, who are hell-bent on power-negotiating everything they buy, trying to get more for less, regardless of the value of the service and in spite of the fact that the businessperson with whom they're negotiating is ten years old! These people make me angry, and I usually tell them so.

The Chiseler

I expect that your daughter will be providing an excellent service or product in her business venture. But if not, the customer has a right to insist that the problem be fixed before he pays for the job.

But sometimes your young entrepreneur will encounter someone who is never satisfied. The weeding in the garden isn't quite perfect, or the garage floor needs to be swept again . . . and again.

No matter how hard your daughter tries, the customer asks for more, demands that he pay less than the agreed-upon price, or even asks for a refund. This has nothing to do with the actual work performed but is instead a way to get out of paying a fair price, or sometimes any price, for the service he received.

The Deadbeat

The most likely difficulty your child will encounter in his or her business is the occasional person who simply doesn't pay up. This happens when the product or service is provided prior to payment being received, often the case in the service businesses your child is likely to start.

Also potentially troublesome is that when your child is just starting out, many of his customers are friends of his or of his parents. When these people are also social friends, collecting what's owed him can be sticky: the parent of the child whom your daughter has taught to swim keeps "forgetting" her checkbook when she brings her son to the pool; a neighbor says he'll "catch you next time" when he picks up his car from your house after your son has washed it; the friend of your wife ordered cookies from your daughter but doesn't have any cash "on hand" to pay for them when your daughter delivers them.

This can be an honest oversight, but it can sometimes also be that your daughter or son has encountered a deadbeat.

Get Savvy with Losers

The great temptation as a parent, when your daughter reports back to you that Mrs. Griffith keeps forgetting to pay her, or your son tells you that the man down the street blames him for breaking his ancient lawn mower and won't pay him, is to pick up the phone and call the customer yourself, or to tell your young entre-preneur to cut his losses and drop the customer. Instead, look on these problems as teaching opportunities. Your future million-aire is going to face customers like these throughout his business career—why not learn to handle them now? Rather than taking over yourself, you can in most cases guide him to successfully negotiate with troublesome clients himself. If he's the one who resolves a problem with the irascible neighbor who doesn't like the way his car was washed, he will be way ahead of the game as an adult businessman, confident and able to handle problems as they come along.

The first rule of business is this: the hardest thing in the world to get is a customer, so when you get someone interested in your product, a good businessperson must try very hard to make the sale.

When a customer throws up roadblocks to your child's suc-cess, here are some strategies you can suggest to him to get the money owed him.

Show Support

As you teach your son coping skills for dishonest customers, also make sure he knows the problems aren't his fault. Let him know that difficult people are out there and that he shouldn't take it personally when the power tripper, the chiseler, and the deadbeat are at their games.

As you go over the strategies that follow, do some role-playing with him so he is comfortable and prepared for what could be some unpleasant conversations. Once he has memorized these preplanned responses, he will know how to keep these problem customers at bay and will gain enormous confidence when he resolves disagreements on his own. And, of course, he will keep more money in his pocket!

Sell the Product

When a customer tries to knock down the price for a product, your son should remind him of the value of his service. What does he provide that's better than his competitors? Maybe his lemonade is sold in larger cups; or when he washes cars, he vacuums the trunk; or he provides the convenience of home delivery of his cookies. Familiarity with the specifics of his product reflects professionalism and confidence in his business. The customer will understand what he's paying for.

Negotiate

To close a deal, your daughter will sometimes have to negotiate with a customer. When a customer suggests a reduced price, she can offer to the split the difference—she's charging $10, the customer suggests $5, and your child agrees on $8, as long as she's not losing money on the deal.

But your future millionaire should never give something away for nothing. If your daughter agrees to do the job for a reduced price, then she should get something in return—permission to post a sign in the customer's front yard, advertising her lawn mowing service; the names of three people she could call to solicit business; or a commitment to a future repeat purchase.

Apologize

If a customer is unhappy with a job or a product, even if he is totally wrong, your son should apologize and say that he's very sorry the customer isn't satisfied. There are a couple of good reasons for this. Most of the time, very difficult customers are unhappy people who thrive on trying to make others unhappy, and you want to keep your son from being sucked into the maelstrom.

Another reason to apologize is that it is never, ever worth it to make the customer mad. A happy customer will tell a friend that he's happy with a service, but an unhappy person will tell ten people what a terrible job your child did, whether it is true or not.

Depending on the circumstances, your son can offer to redo the job, perform the next job at a reduced price, or give the customer something for free, such as a second glass of lemonade. There's some wiggle room here, as he shouldn't have to spend hours cleaning out a garage for the second time if a customer is unreasonably picky, but with experience, your future millionaire will get a sense of what's fair and will not be taken advantage of.

What your child shouldn't do, unless absolutely necessary, is give a refund, because the product/service has a lower cost than the actual cash he receives for the job—the cash includes his profit. So it's always cheaper to give away more product or service, unless too much time is involved, and keep the cash, which is the profit you have built into the service.

Insist on Payment

Your child should never be embarrassed to ask for what's owed her. She has worked hard at her business and deserves prompt payment. If someone doesn't have the money to pay on completion of a service or delivery of an order of, say, T-shirts, your future millionaire should be specific in setting up the time when she can expect to be paid. She should ask when she can come by to pick up the money and insist, politely, on having the customer sign an IOU for the amount due. Also a good idea is to withhold as much of the product/service as possible until full payment can be made. Otherwise, she has given her customer no real incentive to pay her quickly.

If she doesn't get paid when she's supposed to, she should call and remind the customer. It might be uncomfortable for your child to do this, especially with adults, but it's important that she learns to stand up for herself and get what's owed her. She needs this self-confidence as she moves into the business world. Here is where role-playing helps so that she knows exactly what to say.

Sometimes none of this works, however, and your child still can't get paid, which brings me to one of the unpleasant facts of business life—the write-off. If a customer is reminded three times and still hasn't paid, your daughter's chances of getting the money due are slim to none, and you're both better off not wasting any more time. Just move on to the next customer. Every business has unexpected losses, and a business owner has to expect and absorb them when they come along. The phrase "cut your losses" has real meaning. It means to stop spending more time and effort that could be better spent making more sales, more business. Your future millionaire might as well learn this early.

Make a Call

On rare occasions, you must step in to stand up for your son or daughter with a particularly difficult customer. Almost all adults are sensitive in dealing with children, but there are always a few tough nuts who treat children in the same abusive way they treat other adults. When this happens, it's time for you to take over, to even the playing field so that the fight is between two adults.

You'll know when this is appropriate because your son has done everything possible to rectify a situation and is still on the receiving end of unpleasant and unfair accusations.

A phone call or visit without the child will bring the problem to a head. It's unlikely that you will resolve anything, because an unreasonable person is not going to let this happen, but you can at least help your son get out of a bad situation and move on. Important here is to keep your wits about you and

BUSINESS PITFALLS

refuse to let a negative situation spiral out of control. Despite your understandable frustration and anger (how could anyone treat your child this way?), remain professional and calm. It may go your way, and it may not. By remembering that this is just business, you will keep things in perspective and will set a good example for your child.

Get-Rich-Quick Scams

No matter how many times you repeat the mantra "If something seems too good to be true, it probably is," it is human nature to be tempted by the lure of easy money, which is why there's never a shortage of schemes and scams to lure gullible people to part with their hard-earned cash.

The sooner your future millionaire develops a healthy skepticism about business opportunities that don't sound right, the better prepared she will be to identify businesses that are promising and will bring in good money.

There are several ways to guide your daughter to a realistic assessment of business plans without squelching her optimism, including teaching her to rely on her good instincts and pointing out the flaws in some common scams.

Encourage Common Sense

When I was nine years old, there was a boy in my class who always had a pack of gum, was always chewing it, but would never, ever share it. When I smelled his Juicy Fruit gum, my mouth would water, but he would never give a stick away.

Then one day, he offered me some gum. I was ecstatic. Gum! But as I reached out my hand to take it, I suddenly paused. This boy, who never shared anything, seemed much too excited and happy to be giving me his gum. Something told me to pull my hand back and decline his offer, which I did. Then he offered the gum to a friend, and when my friend reached for it—*bzzzz*—he got a little shock from what turned out to be a trick gum pack.

The little bell that went off in my head was the common sense that every kid has about what's reasonable and right. If you can nurture that "gut feeling" in your daughter when looking at business opportunities, she will avoid making financial mistakes. Encourage her to come to you when she has some questions about a project that sounds interesting so that you can walk through it together to see if it's legitimate. Never make her feel stupid when she does. She doesn't have the many years of life experience you have, so be patient and tender as you help her see what seems wrong with this "opportunity." She will steadily build up her defenses as she benefits from your insightful explanations.

Avoid Scams

If you look in the back of any magazine, you will see ads for businesses that promise easy money. "Earn $1,000/week at home and only work a few hours a day," "Millions to be made in real estate," and so on. Very persuasively written, most promise riches if you will only send in money for the materials you need to start.

Almost all of these offers are, if not outright scams, very dubious propositions.

When I had my radio show, *The DunnDeal Show*, we had a feature every week called "White-Collar Investigation." For this segment, we would send away for information about a seemingly bulletproof business opportunity that we found advertised in a magazine. Then we would give it to a successful businessman—

someone with a proven record of performance—and ask him to look into the offer and see if he could make any money.

Ninety-nine percent of the time he came up short. There was little or no real "opportunity" for an entrepreneur—the only money to be made was by the person who placed the ad and collected the $19.95 for the start-up costs.

It's your job to guide your son through these tempting offers and help him understand that most of them are not worth his time. Impress upon him instead that his own ideas and hard work are far more likely to yield him the profits he wants.

Teach him that "the name of the game is to trust your own brain!"

Skip the Lottery

The most widespread scam operating today isn't in the back pages of magazines, but in every deli, newspaper store, and gas station in the country—lottery land.

I can be somewhat annoying on this topic—my wife has been known to walk out of the deli when there's a long line of people buying lottery tickets because she's anticipating my outburst— but lotteries are a terrible, terrible disservice to the average person trying to get ahead financially.

It's one thing when people of means drop a few dollars every month on tickets, but entirely another when people living from paycheck to paycheck throw hard-earned, much-needed money every week at the lottery in the hope of hitting the jackpot.

Unfortunately, according to *MSN Money* the 20 percent of players who contribute 82 percent of lottery revenue are disproportionately low-income, minority men, people least able to afford even small purchases.

Let's say you spend $5 weekly on lottery tickets—$13,000 in fifty years. If you instead invest that amount weekly in a Roth IRA, with a fixed 5.09% annual interest rate, you would yield $59,698.35 after fifty years. Compare that certain income to the odds of winning the Powerball lottery, which are 1 in 121 million!

Your future millionaire should learn as early as possible not to waste even a few dollars on lottery tickets. Teach her instead to invest in her own hopes and dreams, where the payoffs are real and ongoing.

Do Homework

There is help for your future millionaire in protecting himself from bogus businesses. First, he can go to my Web site— YoungBucks.biz—for information aimed at children to help them spot scams and show them how to protect themselves and their businesses from trouble. More generally, the Better Business Bureau—www.bbb.org—offers updated information on scams as well as the means to check on a specific business.

ELEVEN

Sweet Returns on Passive Revenue

MAKE MONEY DO THE WORK

As your future millionaire gets some business experience and money in his pocket, it's time to teach him (and maybe yourself!) that building substantial wealth must include creating revenue when he's not working. Imagine a business that can make your child money while he is at school or football practice! This is a business principle called *passive revenue*.

What exactly is passive revenue? It sounds like lazy money—cash that just lies around and yawns—but it is just the opposite. It is money that does your work for you, when you are busy elsewhere. Stock investing is probably the best-known example of passive revenue. You purchase shares of stock in a company, and when the company prospers (hopefully) and the price of the shares goes up, you sell your shares at the higher price and pocket the profit. The money you earned required no active work on your part—all you had to do was check the stock price from time to time, which is why it's called *passive* revenue.

While the stock market is one way to earn passive income, it is not the only way to generate this type of revenue, nor is it a practical option for most future millionaires who are just beginning to create wealth. So I'd like you to help your son or daughter understand passive income in terms of his or her own businesses.

Work Exchanges Time for Money

Many people define "income" as the money you get when you exchange work for time. This is the most common way to create revenue. When a doctor sees a patient in his office for a half hour, he receives a fee. A factory worker gets paid by the hour. But when either of these workers spends an hour on the golf course, that individual is off the payroll and earns no money. In the same way, your daughter makes money when she sits at her table in front of the supermarket, pouring out glasses of her special lemonade, but doesn't make a dime when she packs up her card table and goes home.

To increase income, most people exchange more hours for more money. The factory employee works overtime on the weekends at time and a half; the doctor extends his office hours and sees more patients. But because there are only twenty-four hours a day, there's a limit to how much a person can earn this way, and it's just not enough to become truly wealthy.

Spending too much time working also throws a person's life out of whack. When an adult works long hours, he has less time for his personal life, which can take a terrible toll on his family. He's not around for a school play, forgets his wedding anniversary, or is too tired to play catch with his son on Saturday morning. Believe me, no success in life can compensate for failure in the home.

The same time/work restraints apply to your future millionaire. Most kids are just as busy as adults. Schoolwork, sports, hobbies, church, and social life take up most of their time, which is the way it should be for children. So your daughter will at some point face the same dilemma that adults do in her business career, which is how to earn more money without spending so much time that she can't do the things she enjoys.

This, I'm happy to report, is entirely possible when you learn how to generate passive income.

Passive income is a combination of two things: (1) creating businesses that generate profits long after you have built the business, and (2) making the money you've earned work for you to make *more* money.

Bill Gates isn't the rich man he is today because he goes to the office from Monday to Friday and builds each computer he sells. When you eat a Mrs. Fields chocolate chip cookie, you can be pretty sure that Debbi didn't bake it herself. But both of them continue to earn lots and lots of money from their businesses and have used their profits to create more wealth.

Following the same model, your eleven-year-old can begin to create passive income almost as soon as he achieves some business success. In doing so, he will be way ahead of his peers in creating wealth and ensuring himself financial independence. Why not start now teaching him to keep the money rolling in while he's rollerblading?

Money Can Work Overtime

Your son is having fun earning some money from a business that he started—with some help from you. Most likely, he's also begun to think about other components of business—how much time he can or wants to spend on the business, how much he can expect to earn from what he's doing and what he wants to do next, and so on.

This is when you can explain to him how to increase his profits without spending any more time on his business.

Hire Employees

Your daughter has followed the steps we outlined in earlier chapters—found a business that interested her, created a market for it, set a reasonable price for her services, and so on—and is now earning good money from walking the neighborhood dogs. In fact, because she's prompt, courteous, and reliable, she has gotten so many customer referrals that not only can she walk dogs every morning and every afternoon after school, but she can also take care of them while their owners are away for the weekend or on longer vacations. She loves dogs and is earning plenty of money, but she's run out of time and tells you that she either has to say no to future customers or has to skip trying out for the school play. She doesn't have time to do both.

Now's the time to introduce her to the most common way for entrepreneurs to generate passive income—employees. She needs to hire another worker—her brother or sister or another neighborhood child—to help her walk the dogs. She will still be in charge of the business (finding customers, handling the schedules and the money) and be ultimately responsible for making sure the dogs are well taken care of, but by paying someone else to walk the dogs she doesn't have time for, she will continue to see her business grow and still have some time for herself. She will be making money while she's rehearsing for the play, just like Bill Gates, who runs his nonprofit foundation while he pays someone else to manufacture his computers!

Many small businesses that could be started by your child, lend themselves to employees, from car washing to cookie baking. Expanding his business this way will teach him to be a good boss.

When he grows up, he'll run his own company with the same efficiency and success.

Sell on Someone Else's Time

Your future millionaire can also generate passive income when he creates a product and someone else sells it. A neighbor's daughter here in Florida has created a great passive-revenue business for herself. Our local airport has a shop with a year-round Christmas display, and Christy sells them Christmas ornaments that she makes from beach shells. Visitors to Florida love to take home souvenirs—and what says "Florida" more than a shell from the beach? Christy loves collecting them on her family's frequent outings to the ocean. At home, she cleans them and decorates them with colorful trinkets and then puts a hook in each one so it can be hung on a tree. Finally, she sends or delivers the pretty shells to the shop, which pays her a tidy sum for her product. Then it's back to the beach for more swimming and shell collecting, while the store sells her ornaments!

Personalized T-shirts sold at the school bookstore, homemade cookies, or hand-picked blueberries on display at the local general store are all possible sources of passive income for your young entrepreneur. Once he gets into the swing of these kinds of earnings, he will become creative and excited about thinking of more ways to create wealth for himself without being on the scene.

Create Your Own Sales

Another source of passive revenue is one-time sales, and your future millionaire should always be on the lookout for opportunities. Not all sales have to be channeled through a store—a young entrepreneur can sell some things on his own.

When I was a boy, my dad and I bought a used Chevy Malibu

for about two hundred dollars. It ran pretty well but looked terrible. Over two Saturday afternoons, we cleaned it up by getting new wheels, washing it, tinting the windows, adding seat covers, installing a tape deck, and so on. When it gleamed like new, we parked it in the driveway with a For Sale sign.

It sat there for about a month, and lots of people saw the car and my sign while I went to school, played football, and did my homework. We got a couple of offers and then sold it for five times what we paid for and put into it.

We had spent only about eight or nine hours fixing up the car and no time selling it other than the five minutes it took me to make the sign! Your future millionaire can prime himself to be alert to projects that don't take too much of his time and can sell themselves. I get new ideas from kids all around the world every day, and when I do, I post them at YoungBucks.biz, so check there frequently for new and interesting ideas.

Turn Money into More Money

Your industrious future millionaire will at some point find that his enterprises have brought him some tidy profits. He's bought the MP3 player that first motivated him to start earning his own money and still has cash to burn. If he's to become truly wealthy, however, he needs to understand the second component of passive income: sitting on his pile of money and counting it daily might be very satisfying but is a bad idea if he wants to become a millionaire.

People tend to think of money as a rock—a solid, unchanging pile that is always there to support you. But, unfortunately, that's not true. Money does not stay the same in terms of value. It is always moving, either shrinking or growing, and your future millionaire has to grasp this principle, which I call "dying dollars." If he doesn't invest his money to keep it growing, his dollars will slowly decrease in value, or "die." Young entrepreneurs must understand this before they wake up in twenty-five years and discover that they have less and less money every day and have lost twenty-five years of opportunity.

This is a tough concept to get across to children who have been weaned on squirreling away their coins in piggy banks, but I've discovered that the best way to jump-start them into investing their earnings is to tell them this:

Think of your money as your first employee.

A good boss pays attention to what his employees do, encouraging them to perform at their best and making sure they are earning the money he pays them. He should do exactly the same with the money he's earned. Don't let it sit in the bank; get it back in circulation so that it creates more money.

Keep Money Busy

Following are a number of ways for your future millionaire to generate more profits from the money he's earned. Younger children will need more hands-on guidance than older children, but all ages can profit from these learn-to-earn suggestions.

Reinvest in Your Business

Investors are always warned against putting too much money into one stock or company. But what better place for your future millionaire to put his extra profits than back into the successful business in which he earned them in the first place? He has already proven that the business is a good one, so why not make it grow? He can buy a more efficient mower to mow lawns more quickly or increase his next order of the T-shirts he sells, both of which will increase his profits and net worth without taking more of his time.

Start a New Business

Remember when you had your first business meeting with your daughter to talk about all the businesses she could start? Most likely she probably had more than one idea that interested her. Well, now that her first business is successful, takes up less of her time, and is bringing in extra money that needs to be put to work, she can go back and revisit that original list of business ideas and perhaps start a second one!

Buy Real Estate

Older children who have been working for a number of years at various businesses can accumulate quite a nest egg, so investing in real estate is not the pie-in-the-sky idea you might think. Rather than buying a car as soon as a large amount of money has been earned, consider buying a house! You and your future millionaire probably know your community as well or better than any investor and can find properties in up-and-coming neighborhoods where you're likely to make a healthy profit when you sell. One increasingly viable plan for college students is to buy a condo (often with other students), live in it while getting a degree, and then, after graduating, sell it to incoming students at a nice profit. For a reasonable down payment, your young financier can own rather than rent, building equity. A side benefit is that he or she will also learn how to take care of a house.

Buying real estate requires an adult to cosign mortgages or to take title of the property, and my YoungBucks.biz site contains the information you need to know when making this type of investment.

Be "the Bank"

Lending money to others is a very good way to generate passive revenue. But it can also cause hurt feelings among friends and family, so this idea should be pursued very carefully. There are other very nice people who, for numerous reasons, cannot get traditional financing for such things as cars, home improvements, electronics, and so on. Your future millionaire can put some of his money to work by earning interest from someone who needs a loan and has the income to pay. (I have included a sample loan document that you can download and modify at YoungBucks.biz.)

During my brief stint in college, I became "the bank" in my dorm for friends who ran out of money on the weekends. Because of my businesses, I always had cash around, and my friends would borrow money from me. I charged them interest on the loan and also asked for collateral, usually their stereos, to make sure I got paid back. I made quite a bit of money and even kept a stereo when a guy left college before paying me back and never returned to the campus. I sold that, too, and made some more money!

Spread the word that you can finance small purchases for a reasonable rate of interest and you will find yourself earning extra money with no effort. Set up a formal system, keeping written copies of your agreements. Also make sure you know and trust your customers, and insist on some collateral. You can't depend on wise guys to get your loan repaid.

Investing in Stocks

If your young entrepreneur is a preteen or older, you can introduce her to stock investing. There are many books about investing in the stock market that you and your future millionaire can read to become familiar with this type of sophisticated passive income. I have also asked my own personal financial advisor to put together some tips and stock ideas for future millionaires, and he updates them every week at YoungBucks.biz.

Shares are usually sold in blocks, which may be beyond the budget of most young entrepreneurs, but it is possible to buy one or two shares of some stocks. Encourage your daughter to buy one share of a company that she knows and likes, from Disney to Wal-Mart to Toys-R-Us, and then the two of you can spend time together every week or month tracking the company's progress so she becomes comfortable with profit and loss. Eventually those purchases will get larger, as will the dividends!

TWELVE

YoungBucks.biz

CONTINUE THE JOURNEY WITH ME

YOU AND I HAVE JUST COVERED A LOT OF TERRITORY AND embarked on a very exciting journey on behalf of your children. You are now light-years ahead of the vast majority of parents in the world when it comes to raising a future millionaire. Don't stop now!

Young Bucks is an essential primer for guiding your children to a new way of thinking about money, business, and their own success. But it is only the beginning. Just as important as starting your child in his first business is helping him continue to enjoy new experiences and discoveries and learn to overcome the inevitable hurdles and pitfalls that every businessperson faces. You cannot do this alone.

As you have read *Young Bucks* and begun to teach your child how to start his first business, you may have already wished that there was someone you could talk to about this adventure—perhaps you wanted some advice on how to approach your child or needed some suggestions for dealing with a difficult situation that cropped up with one of your son's customers, or maybe you would have liked to brainstorm with another parent of an entrepreneur about some business ideas. But since what you've been learning is so different from what most parents teach their children about money and business, you probably found it difficult to find fellow travelers who could share your enthusiasm about what your kids are discovering. Well, now you can.

Web Site World

My Web site, YoungBucks.biz, is specifically designed for you—and for the thousands of parents I have worked with over the years—to make sure that you have all the information and backup you need to continue to help your future millionaires thrive. It is the logical next step for you to take to consolidate what you have taught your child and to keep him or her interested in and informed about the exciting world of being an entrepreneur.

My goal is ambitious—I want to involve you in the largest gathering of like-minded parents there ever was so that together we can share and promote the life-changing transformations that come with guiding children to self-confidence and business success. Why not? There are large national and even international support groups for people who share common interests or burdens, from people who feel strongly about everything from politics to NASCAR racing to alcoholism, and each provides information and practical and emotional support to its members. Time and time again, the success of these organizations has proved how powerfully group dynamics can generate change. People tend to lose more weight in weight-loss groups. People have a higher success of overcoming an addiction when supported by others who have traveled the same journey. Political organizations reaching out on the Web can bring change to the electorate. Even chat rooms on NASCAR can affect opinions and thoughts!

YoungBucks.biz offers exactly the same access for parents like you, who are committed to helping their children achieve financial success. The site allows you to share your son's life-changing adventures with other parents who will be supportive of your efforts, eager to hear your advice, and equally excited to report on their own children's businesses and experiences.

The success I've enjoyed in my businesses is a direct result of the wonderful community I've been a part of for my whole life, beginning at the coffee counter at Denny's with my dad and continuing with the many entrepreneurs and businesspeople I've known. All of these people have helped me with excellent ideas, strategies, contacts, and, equally important, emotional support, encouragement, and friendship. In fact, I would not have achieved what I have been able to accomplish without this network of like-minded, energetic, and generous souls.

You deserve no less.

Advice and Support

As a new member of our online community, you will benefit greatly from the many years of experience and insight that other parents are sharing through our message boards, blogs, and newsletters. Ongoing support, guidance, and information are crucial to building on what you've started by reading *Young Bucks*. In this way you can grow as a mentor, and your child can grow as a future millionaire. And you will have a tremendous amount of fun while you do it.

YoungBucks.biz is not only a community of parents just like yourselves, but also includes advice from investors, media folks, and other support personnel who share your passion to help children realize their personal and financial dreams. These professionals join me in providing an enormous amount of specific information for parents interested in guiding their children to business success. I guarantee that the answer to almost any business question you have is available at this Web site. YoungBucks.biz is a wonderful resource that gets better every day as more parents like you get involved.

Additionally, I am constantly on the lookout for new business ideas for kids as well as ways to develop new financial resources for them and create new events and opportunities to increase their personal network and their overall success. All of this information goes directly to YoungBucks.biz.

The Boomerang Effect

One of the main reasons that YoungBucks.biz is so successful is the generosity of its members, who offer as much help to others as they receive from the Web site. As anyone knows who has donated money to charity or time to a service organization, giving is as important, if not more important, than getting, because in enriching others you enrich yourself beyond measure. People aren't just being polite when they say they received far more than they gave in their volunteering experience—it's true! It has been my personal experience that no matter how much of my time or money I contribute to a worthy cause or a needy individual, it comes back to me in abundance.

This is how YoungBucks.biz works too—what you contribute to the Web site comes right back to you, like a boomerang tossed in the air. This is what differentiates the site from many other entrepreneurial organizations. The last result I want from helping your children unleash their tremendous earning power is to be blamed twenty years down the road for helping create an entirely new group of millionaires who are selfish with their wealth. Because of the site's emphasis on the importance of giving as good as you get, children at YoungBucks.biz learn the importance of balance and generosity in the pursuit of wealth.

My own commitment to the Web site includes taking the time—several times weekly—to personally answer questions from parents who are seeking additional insight or further clarification. I very much enjoy my Web site "chats" with excited parents. And you will be able to contribute as well.

You may not believe this now, but you are on your way to becoming an expert. As time passes and you and your child launch new businesses, you will have newfound knowledge and life experiences to pass along to others. When that happens—and you will know it when you start nodding at information on the Web site that is familiar, and you have already made it a part of your business guide for your child—I ask you to take the time to reach out to parents who have just begun to help their children and pass along the tips and advice that will help them successfully navigate the road you have traveled. Generously sharing good advice and business tips with others generates even more ideas and energy and is a rising tide that lifts all boats.

A Peek Inside

Easy to navigate, YoungBucks.biz has a parents' section for you and another for your children. The parents' section continues the work introduced in *Young Bucks*, providing more business strategies and opportunities for your young entrepreneur. In addition, it includes forums for you to chat directly with other parents, including me!

Your child can also enjoy the site, finding info about businesses he would like, swapping stories with other entrepreneurs from all over the country, and making new friends with young businesspersons who share his interests and goals.

The Web site will act as an ongoing mentor for you so that you can remain informed, enthusiastic, and supportive of your future millionaire. So log on and continue on the journey with many, many parents like you, who believe in their children and want to help them be all that they can be. Here is some of the information that parents and young entrepreneurs will find on YoungBucks.biz:

- A regularly updated database of new business ideas for children, including those from my own experience as well as successful enterprises from other parents. You can add your own ideas and experiences here, which will be resources for other parents to use in helping their children market and promote their businesses. Included is information about press releases, advice on contacting the media, e-mail marketer resources, marketing articles, and tips from industry pros. I also provide templates for business cards, letterhead stationery, and simple contracts.

- Community networking boards—one for parents and one for kids. Parents can meet here to talk business, network for their children, share resources, or even set up business partnerships! Young entrepreneurs can in the same way talk to their peers, enjoying the company of ambitious and successful people like themselves.

- Capital Corner. This unique section will link future millionaires to investors and venture capitalists who want to invest in the business opportunities of young entrepreneurs. Not everyone wants to give their money to the state lottery!

- Free legal advice. I have on tap several lawyers who volunteer their services to assist young entrepreneurs in the legal aspects of setting up their businesses, including help setting up a corporation.

- Talk to Me! I love talking to Young Bucks directly. Members of the Web site can ask me questions in a chat room and also see what advice I've given others. I enjoy talking to future millionaires and their parents and can offer lots of help from my years of business experience with young people. This direct access is available only through YoungBucks.biz.

- *DunnDeal* Magazine/E-newsletter. This monthly online publication includes hot tips, such as news about a successful new business from one town that can be effectively replicated in another community; investor resources—places entrepreneurs can go for funding for new businesses; profiles of successful Young Bucks; and media opportunities.

   The media, including those reporters, directors, and producers in television, radio, newspapers, and the Web, use YoungBucks.biz as a resource when looking for news stories about young entrepreneurs. The newsletter reports these media opportunities, and the resulting stories are priceless in promoting your child's business venture.

- Calendar. There are numerous events for young entrepreneurs all over the world—conferences, trade shows, and so on. Check out this calendar for venues that might interest your son or daughter.

- Scholarships. Numerous scholarship opportunities are available for enterprising future millionaires, as well as business competitions and contests. Look here for an updated listing of these coveted opportunities.

Good-bye and Hello

We have finished the first part of our journey together, and my hope is that you and your child are together enjoying his growing confidence and success as a young entrepreneur. What you are doing for your child may seem fairly practical—teaching him skills so he can comfortably support himself as an adult—but the impact of your attention to him and of your time together is far more profound than you may think.

You are showing him in the most direct way possible how much you respect and believe in his abilities. You are using your own experiences (intermingled with mine) to guide him to the best possible use of those gifts. Finally, you are creating a friendship that will continue throughout your lives.

While the financial rewards of your commitment to your child are tremendous, what you share with him is more important than money. You are passing along to him timeless values that he will take to heart as he moves through his own life and starts his own family. I speak from my own experience. My children and their many businesses and ever-growing, self-funded savings accounts are a direct result of my dad's support and belief in me. And I know that when my kids are grown and have families of their own, their children will grow up to start businesses and develop their dreams into reality. All this time together with my father and my children has meant a great deal to me, far more than the actual dollars and cents earned in pursuit of our various enterprises, although the cash has been very nice!

You and your children will be enriched in the same ways as you continue to work together on entrepreneurial goals. But if you have read this book and seen your child make his first dollar on a business that he created himself, you already know that. My job is done.

Thank you for taking the time to read *Young Bucks*. See you on the Web site!

About the Author

Troy Dunn is a successful entrepreneur, television personality, and motivational speaker who has inspired and entertained millions of people worldwide. His humble and humorous way of communicating principles and values makes him a highly sought-after talk show guest and keynote speaker to corporations and organizations alike.

Troy has hosted a nationally syndicated talk-radio show in eighty-one cities; has authored more than a dozen books and tapes on a variety of teen, marriage, and parenting topics; and even performs a stand-up comedy show called *An Evening with Troy*, which talks about the ups and downs of family life.

Troy is actively engaged in his Christian faith and proudly declares Jesus Christ as his Lord and Savior. Troy has been "blistfully" married to Jennifer, his high school sweetheart, for nineteen years, and they have five sons and two daughters. His favorite charities are those connected with pediatric cancer research, such as the Ronald McDonald House and All Children's Hospital.